Second Shift

Susan Tekulve

Second Shift

Essays by
Susan Tekulve

Del Sol Press
Washington, D.C.

Second Shift
by Susan Tekulve

Published by Del Sol Press
Washington, D.C.

First printing 2018

Cover: Abby McGuire

Printed in the United States of America

ISBN 978-0-9998425-0-8

Thanks to Sarah Gray for her expert proofreading.

To the memory of my mother,
Nancy Joy Tekulve, (1941-2017)

Now you can remember everything. But there's no more time, it's morning, time to go to work, and they are opening the huge shop door, that slow rumble you will never forget, and the light leaking in, widening – light like a quilt of gold foil flung out so it will drape all of this, will keep it and keep it well – and it is so bright now, you can hardly bear it as it fills the door, this immense glacier of light coming on, and still you do not know who you are, but here it is, try to remember, it is all beginning:

– B.H. Fairchild, "The Memory Palace"

Acknowledgements

I would like to thank the editors and staff of the following publications, in which these essays appeared:

"Second Shift," *Web Del Sol*; republished in *Writers On the Job*, Hopewell Publications

"The Peach Season," *Still: The Journal*

"The Plain of Sorrento," *Puerto del Sol*

"Loitering in a Field of Confederate Dead," *Creative Loafing*

"Following the Slow Black River," *The Louisville Review*

"Hell Broth and Poisoned Entrails; An Affair With Scottish Cookery," *The Book of Worst Meals*, Serving House Books

"Survivors," *The South Carolina Review*

"Silent Song," *Appalachian Heritage*

My thanks to Walter Cummins and Thomas E. Kennedy for their enduring enthusiasm and generous support of my writing over many years; to my husband, Rick, whose vision helped me find my way through this book; to my musician son, Hunter, who listened to me read most of these essays aloud; to everybody who made time to read early versions of these essays, especially Rachel Hall, Thomas E. Kennedy, and Jon Sealy; and to Jason Howard and Karen McElmurray, gracious editors and writers who gently insisted I start showing my nonfiction to the world.

This book is dedicated to my mother, who put the very first book in my hands, and taught me how to read it.

Contents

Second Shift

WHEN I WAS ACCEPTED INTO MIAMI UNIVERSITY, my grandfather agreed reluctantly to help with tuition, though I would need to work part-time for my board and living expenses. Miami University is a beautiful old campus. Ancient maples shade its red brick buildings, and there is a copper pendulum that swings in front of the academic hall where I took my first college English course in early American literature. That fall, I'd sit in the shade of this giant pendulum, reading Melville, Hawthorne, Thoreau, and Emerson. I'd always been a reader. All through my childhood, I read my mother's high school English books — *Jane Eyre*, *The Odyssey*, and *Wuthering Heights* — that she kept in an empty rosewood crib down in the basement. I read the ten years of back issues of *National Geographic* my father kept on the shelves beside the crib. That fall, I was pleased that I could earn college credit for reading. I imagined, however, that the pendulum I sat beside was the college clock ticking, and that I must hurry up and choose a major that would lead to a "useful job" when I graduated, something in the medical or teaching field. I had disliked Psychology 101 the most that term, but it seemed like the only class I was taking that would lead to a job that would serve others. I declared a psychology major and told everyone back home that I was studying to become a psychologist.

Friday afternoons, I drove the rural road that led from Oxford, Ohio, back to my hometown of Cincinnati with my best friend, Mary. Her father worked as a paper engineer at the Procter and Gamble factory, and he'd gotten us both second-shift jobs in the detergent division. Every Saturday and Sunday, Mary and I went together to the sprawling factory compound east of Cincinnati, followed a labyrinth of hallways until we entered a lounge crowded with Formica tables and a vending machine filled with P&G food products. At three o'clock, we punched our time cards and pulled surgical masks over our mouths and noses, securing protective glasses over our eyes. Then we entered a smaller room where we sat on high stools around a circular machine to assemble a new Tide product, a combination detergent and softener designed to release the detergent as the washer filled with water, the softener after the first rinse. My fingers grew sticky with the detergent crystals, and my throat became terminally raw from the dust, but I never grew weary or discouraged. I knew this dull work was temporary. After my shift ended, I went home and remained sleepless well past midnight. My thick American literature text cracked open across a pillow on my lap, I read Melville's "Bartleby the Scrivener" or "Life in the Iron Mills" by Rebecca Harding Davis until dawn. I didn't make the connection between myself and the characters who inhabited these stories. They were works of fiction, and I was a college student who was studying to become a psychologist.

During our fifteen-minute break each night, Mary and I shared a package of Pringles and talked. She knew of a job in the deodorant division of P&G that paid eight dollars an hour if you were willing to sniff the underarms of those who were testing the new deodorants. We spent a lot of time pondering how this task was orchestrated. Did one individual stand with her arm raised while the other leaned in and sniffed? How close, exactly, did one have to get to another person's underarm to determine that the product was effective? A week before Christmas, I developed a bronchial cough from the detergent dust that made my chest feel tight and heavy. The more I coughed the worse my chest felt, and my mother feared this would lead to pneumonia, an illness she said had nearly killed me when I was an infant. It wasn't too difficult to convince her that I should quit when the fall term ended.

My mother worked as a secretary for a psychologist who counseled DUI offenders, and over Christmas break she got the idea that I could work with her at the psychologist's office to see if this was the kind of job I wanted to do for the rest of my life. She even arranged an "interview" with her boss, Dr. English, about his field of expertise. One Monday morning, I went with her to the suburban medical complex office that Dr. English shared with his associate, a psychiatrist. In the waiting room, I observed a sad-eyed woman paging listlessly through stacks of *Travel and Leisure* and *Good Housekeeping*. An elderly couple sat in the far corner, heads bent toward each other, the woman clutching a plastic grocery bag filled with prescription bottles. Suddenly the old woman stood, her face filled with anger and mystery. Holding her bag of pills out before her, she walked slowly toward the blue water cooler near the reception desk, and drank cone after paper cone of fountain water. As her husband rushed to guide her back to her seat, my mother hurried me back to the room where she was going to type out DUI reports, and I would file them.

In the back room, the bookshelves were lined with seventeen volumes of Jung's collected works. A fireman puppet was slung over the far corner of the lower shelf, nearly hiding a copy of *Depression and Human Existence*. Taking my seat beside the filing cabinet, I made mental notes to ask Dr. English if he'd read all those thick books, and how he used that puppet for therapy sessions. My mother sat across the room beside a window that overlooked a gravel rooftop, typing out d.u.i reports dictated into a tape recorder by Dr. English. All afternoon I filed to the sound of the psychologist murmuring, "Point zero nine," the click and screech of the tape recorder as my mother turned it off, rewound the tape, listened to the tragic blood alcohol level again.

Two hours and six paper cuts later, my neck ached from hunching over the file cabinet, and I was struggling with the powerful urge to run over to the bookshelf and play with the psychologist's puppet. Though I suspected that the DUI files were confidential, I began reading a few, vaguely looking for information that would help connect this mind-numbing work with my newly chosen career in psychology. First, I read through the police report to find out the blood alcohol level of those sentenced to DUI counseling. Then I read the sheet that recorded how the patients were faring during the mandatory counseling sessions. My mother typed on. Every once in a while, she turned absentmindedly toward me to ask if I needed more file stickers or folders. I'm certain she noticed that I was reading the reports, but she was working to put me through college, and at the moment she wanted me out of her hair so that she could finish her typing. Soon, I stopped filing completely and just read.

Near the end of the "L" files, I spotted a familiar name, the father of a boy I'd gone to high school with. The police report said this man had wrapped his Buick around a Buckeye tree just down the street from where we lived. When they got to him, he was trying to start the car back up. He kept turning the key in the ignition like he was going to drive away.

I know him, I thought as I reread the file. I know his family. It was a sad revelation, but I could not make the connection between that tragic blood alcohol level and all that Zeitgeist theory from Psychology 101. For that matter, I could not make the connection between anything I'd studied during my one term in psychology and the minds and hearts of those people I'd seen in the eerie waiting room. I stopped reading and began filing until my mother announced that we were done for the evening.

I never got to interview Dr. English about the field of psychology. He forgot about our interview and went home before my mother had a chance to introduce him to me. I went back to school the next week, and began attending the American Literature Part II course I'd enrolled in before leaving for Winter break. I took a job in the cafeteria next to my dorm so that I could stay at school on weekends, working food prep with the full-time help. Women from the farm counties surrounding the campus, they wore immaculate white uniforms, but their hands were stained black from picking tobacco in the summers. Peeling carrots and potatoes, I listened to them discuss their aching backs and feet, their dreams of acquiring comfortable desk jobs in computer data entry. As with my job at the Procter and Gamble factory, I didn't mind the work. I could finish an early morning shift, shower the sour cafeteria smell off my body and still read Faulkner's "Barn Burning" or Robert Frost's "After Apple Picking" before my nine a.m. class.

By the second semester of my sophomore year, I'd taken only one psychology class but had completed half an English major, though I still told everyone I was majoring in psychology. I figured I had two more years to decide on a "useful" major, plenty of time to sign up for that introduction to creative writing course I'd always wanted to take. That spring, I took my first creative writing course with the poet James Reiss, a tall, lanky man with a New York accent. During the first class, he introduced the class to poetic line, sound and concrete imagery. He told us a poem could be about anything. To prove his point, he read the William Carlos Williams poem about the ripe plums and told us all to go home and write a poem about anything.

I went directly back to my dorm. Down in the basement study carrels, I wrote my first poem about my grandmother's bunion surgery. Shortly before she died, my grandmother's bunions had grown so large that she couldn't wear anything but house slippers with the sides cut out. The bunions didn't prevent her from walking, but my grandfather wanted her to have the surgery. He'd grown up in a coldwater flat in the river bottoms, the middle son of Sicilian immigrants, but he'd worked his way into being an accountant who could afford to pay for his American wife's unnecessary foot surgery. Her feet bound after her surgery, my grandmother sat in an armchair before a TV tray, painting tiny violets and roses on tablecloths and bed linens until the end of her life.

The next week, I turned in a free verse poem titled "My Grandmother's Bunions." At the beginning of the following class, Jim Reiss lumbered in with a stack of our poems and read each one aloud, pointing out clichés, their fatal resemblance to rock song lyrics. When he reached my poem, I held my breath until he finished reading and walked over to my desk.

"Bunions!" he said. "Now this is what I mean by concrete detail."

Looking back, it was probably a really bad poem, but the fact that Jim Reiss was able to pull some small gem of encouragement from it was absolutely thrilling. From then on, whenever I was not in my classes, I was down in the basement study carrels scribbling out poems on lined yellow note pads until late into the night. I saw poems in everything, and I began making the connection between my writing course, the literature I was reading, and the life around me. I wrote about how in winter, when my brother's landscaping business was slow, and he plowed snow on the rural roads north of Cincinnati to make a living. He kept a stack of my father's *National Geographics* on the front seat of his truck to hand out to stranded travelers so that they wouldn't get bored and wander out of their cars, die of hypothermia on the side of the road before the police could reach them. I wrote a

15

villanelle told through the voices of the full-time workers in the dorm cafeteria. Every night, I went to my poetry as if it were my second shift job, the kind of work that would sustain me until I achieved my worthier, true occupation. Sinking deeper into the work, I thought only of end-stopped lines and enjambment, sound and rhythms. When I finished a draft of a poem, my whole body ached from hunching too long over a desk, but I felt pleasantly spent, unafraid of where this work was leading.

After the final class with Jim Reiss, I ran back to my dorm room and wept because the class had ended. I read through the course catalogue, discovering that if I took intermediate and advanced poetry workshops I wouldn't have to stop writing. I'd read Hemingway's *In Our Time* and learned that he made a living as a reporter, so I signed up for a journalism class and started writing for the school newspaper. This was during the Reagan era, in the middle of Ohio, and I kept my chosen occupation to myself. Most of my friends were majoring in business or education, and when I mentioned that I was majoring in English they imitated a K-Mart siren and hollered, "Blue light special on aisle seven!" One day after a workshop, Jim Reiss observed that though he liked my poems, they were all narratives. He suggested that I try a fiction class. I took all the fiction writing classes, repeating the advanced fiction workshop twice. In the winter of my senior year, I applied and was accepted into the MFA program in fiction at Wichita State University for the following fall.

To save up for living expenses, I moved back home the summer before graduate school. I didn't have a job. Mary's father had retired from Procter and Gamble after having a stroke our senior year, and I didn't want to bother her family about work at the factory. Dr. English had retired after his associate quit their practice and bought a bar down on the Ohio River, so my mother was in between secretarial jobs and couldn't take me to work with her. Every afternoon she and I sunbathed together on lawn chairs in the back yard, her high school novels from the old crib in the basement stacked between us. As I read *Wuthering Heights* and drank sun tea, my mother talked about all my friends who'd already secured their first "real jobs" in healthcare or education.

My college boyfriend had become a male nurse, and though he'd broken up with me to marry a girl he'd been seeing while we were still dating, my mother mused aloud that he'd chosen an unusual but solid occupation for a man, and that it was a shame things hadn't worked out between us. My mother had kept in touch with my boyfriend's mother, and she knew all about my ex-boyfriend's new fiancée. According to my mother, my ex-boyfriend's fiancée wasn't pretty, but she was the very definition of kindness. An Italian Catholic girl, she worked extra shifts at Good Samaritan hospital as an X-ray technician. Just the week before, she'd found a man lying still on her X-ray table, not breathing, and she'd resuscitated him. Unable to listen to one more word of praise about this good Catholic girl who seemed worthier of my ex-boyfriend than I was, I snapped my book shut and went inside.

The next Sunday, my mother, father and I went to my grandfather's house. He was getting too old to care for the sprawling, brick ranch perched on a slope of land beside a horse farm that boarded the Clydesdale horses that pulled the Budweiser wagon in the downtown parades. While my mother cooked supper, my father and I stayed outside. My father drove a riding mower up and down my grandfather's lawn as I gathered the lopsided green apples that dropped from my grandfather's trees into a wheelbarrow. Then I rolled the apples down to the barbed wire fence at the edge of my grandfather's property, and dumped the fallen fruit over the fence for the wild Shetland ponies that lived in the woods to eat.

My grandfather kept a water cooler on the screened-in porch off his kitchen. On one of my trips up the hill, I went into the porch for a cup of water. My father had stopped the lawn mower to pick up a stick in his path, and in this sudden silence, I heard my grandfather's husky voice coming from the kitchen. Standing beside the kitchen doorway, I saw my dark, straight-backed grandfather pacing behind my mother as she stirred a pot of marinara sauce, layering the lasagna noodles with ricotta and sweet Italian sausage.

"She's outta control," my grandfather said. "What's she gonna do with another degree in poetry?"

"She's studying fiction now," my mother said.

"How much is that gonna cost?"

"She has a teaching assistantship. She'll be earning her tuition and living expenses by teaching."

After a long pause, my grandfather said, "Maybe when she gets this out of her system and stops all her wandering she'll come home and be a teacher." He went into the dining room, opened the top drawer of the hutch where he kept his checkbook. He came back into the kitchen. "It's cold in Kansas." He tore a check from the book. "She'll need a warm winter coat."

Though I'd felt it all along, my grandfather's open disapproval still bothered me. I'd never thought of my choice to study writing in graduate school as rebellious. Thanks to my literature and creative writing classes, I'd been a good student. But now that I'd returned home, I realized that in the eyes of my family I had finished four years of college without acquiring any useful job skills. I had not spent the last four years training to resuscitate dying men on X-ray tables or to teach school children. I knew how to write poems and short stories. This was hard work, but it was selfish work that didn't seem to serve anyone but myself.

At my parents' house that night, I scoured the classifieds for a job. Since I'd come home, I'd begun setting my alarm clock so that I could wake early to read Raymond Carver's stories about vitamin salesmen and dog groomers, Andre Dubus's heartbreaking tales of lonely barmaids. I knew that these writers wrote about the lives they knew, if not about themselves, and I'd read an essay by Carver that said if you want to write a good story you must tell a little secret about yourself. Feeling my own sheltered life was as open as a blank page, I began looking for a second shift job that Carver or Dubus might have worked. I thought that if I brought myself to low places I would be able to write the dark and lovely stories I so admired. I wanted to tell my own dark secrets.

Still stinging from my mother's story about my ex-boyfriend's saintly new fiancée, I found a job as a recreation assistant at a home for the severely mentally retarded. An hour's drive from my parents' house, the home stood like an abandoned elementary school in the middle of a field, surrounded by a warped and rusted chain-linked fence. Hired to stimulate people whose mental development stopped somewhere between the ages of three weeks and a year, I was required to find ways to "speak" to people who knew very few words, to provide exercise for full-grown men and women whose limbs had atrophied so severely that they weighed no more than infants.

This was a place parents took children they wanted to forget. No one was allowed to bring a camera into the facility, but there were mirrors along the hallways and in the individual rooms. It was explained to me that these people needed to recognize themselves in mirrors, to remind themselves that they still existed. I spent the first week shadowing a young woman named Anna who worked as a nurse's aid. While feeding and bathing the individual patients, she called them each by name, identifying their personality quirks and habits for me. "Bernie likes to sit in the hallway where she can watch the clock," she said. She introduced me to a full-grown man whose eyes were full of intelligence, though his arms and legs were curled against his body like the other patients. "Bruce isn't like the others," she said. "He's got some kind of disease in his nervous system. He can't talk much anymore, but he likes it when you talk to him."

The next week, I assumed my post in the recreation room at 8 a.m. and found myself standing in the middle of the floor with a beach ball in my hands, surrounded by people in wheelchairs. Some of the patients slept while others waited, their eyes locked on me. Though their bodies were as helpless as newborns, their faces had aged and hardened, and as I looked into their eyes I knew they understood loneliness and hard use well beyond their official IQs. I thought of the young woman who'd trained me the week before. I marveled at how easily she'd spoken to them, rocking them in her arms as though they were her own children. I went into the supply closet and stood for a very long time.

Surrounded by shelves of athletic equipment and padded floor mats, I thought of Saint Catherine nursing the lepers. I remembered the mystical saying taught to me in Catholic grade school, "Know that you are she who is not." I knew only that I was not a saint, and that I wasn't cut out for this kind of work. But I was determined to prove to everyone that I was able to do something remotely useful, and selfless. I brought out a boom box and beanbag and rolled the sleeping patients into patches of sunlight near the window. I pulled the ones who remained awake into a close circle. I turned on the boom box, and gave one of the patients who could hold things the beanbag. We played an improvised version of hot potato, with me passing the "potato" for the ones who couldn't until it was time for my shift to end, and I could go home.

About a month after I took the job at the nursing home, my mother came into my bedroom one morning, carrying a small, blue suitcase. She'd surprised me with this suitcase when I eight, the first time I slept over at my grandparents' house. I'd loved this suitcase, and when I wasn't using it for sleepovers, I filled it with my favorite books and journals, and carried it everywhere with me. The suitcase bulged, and when I opened it all the stories and poems I'd written in high school spilled out across my lap. When I asked my mother why she'd saved them, she shrugged, "You were always writing. I remember all your stories." She also gave me a manila envelope filled with clips of my college news stories I'd mailed to her. She suggested that I choose a couple of my best ones to send off to a few newspapers and ask for work as a reporter. The next week, I got a call from the editor of a local weekly who said she could use a stringer to write features, that she'd pay twenty dollars a story, an extra eight if I took the photos.

Working as a reporter, I was able to write about everything around me once again – as long as everything happened in the farm counties above the Ohio River, on the east side of Cincinnati. Every Monday, I went to the bureau and paged through the black binder my editor filled with press releases, looking for subjects that would make good human-interest stories. I interviewed the Buckeye United Fly Fishermen, a group of men devoted to fly-fishing. The only trout-sustaining stream in Ohio was near Upper Sandusky, about six hours away, so they spent much of their time talking about fishing and the art of fly tying, and they were eager to share this knowledge with me. I spent another afternoon with a troop of Civil War re-enactors called The Army of Ohio who drilled in a soggy cow pasture down the road from Saint Rita's School for the Deaf. I spent so much time with my sources that it took days to type up my notes, determine my angle and what material I actually needed to put in the stories. Every Friday, I met with my editor, Jean, in her office. She made suggestions for cuts, reminding me of narrow newspaper columns, the need for advertising space. Then she gave me the letters written by sources who wanted to thank me for writing their stories. At summer's end, Jean offered me a full-time job working the education beat. Though I turned it down, I was tempted. It was the first job that had shown me how necessary my writing could be to others.

In Wichita, after my parents helped move my chest of drawers and bed into my tiny apartment, there wasn't much room for them to sleep. They booked a hotel room that night, and promised to return before seven the next morning to say goodbye before driving back to Ohio, but they didn't arrive at my apartment until 11 a.m. the next day. My mother stood on the porch with me while my father walked to the back of the van, pulled out a large, white box.

"Did you guys sleep in?" I said.

"Your father wanted to visit a hardware store," my mother said.

"She needed a table," my father said as he carried the box into my apartment.

The box was filled with many parts of a small, oak table that required assembling. He overturned the table's top, set it on the floor of my kitchen, lining the four legs beside it. Then he sliced open a plastic bag of metal corner braces, screws and dowels. He brought out a brown hardware store sack filled with wood glue and a planing tool he'd bought especially for the occasion. He didn't open the directions. The assembly, which should have taken an hour, ended at 2 p.m. when my mother told my father that he must finish up, they still had a long drive ahead of them. My father turned the table upright, set the level on its top, gave it a critical look and rocked the table with one hand to test its strength. He shook his head, turned the table upside down again, but my mother looked at her watch.

"She needs a table," my father said fiercely, but he turned the table upright again. His shoulders sagged, and when I knelt beside him to help pick up the spare brackets and screws off the floor, I saw that his eyes were red. "You won't be coming home again," he said softly.

"It's a fine table," I said. "I'm coming home for Christmas."

That night after my parents left, I placed my Smith Corona on the table my father had built and hung my new winter coat in the closet. I was finally alone, but I wasn't lonely. Soon, I began meeting teachers and students who wanted to write as badly as I did. I began learning how to teach college English so that I could support myself and, ideally, have time to practice my craft. About a month into the term, I wrote my first published short story. I'd been thinking about how to tell this story for weeks, but it came to me late one night when I wasn't actually writing, and I ran to my oak table in the kitchen to write it all down.

A good teacher once told me that the only difference between writing and any other job is that a writer is someone who writes. Though it is an art form, writing is not a lofty process. You must go to it every day, steadily and faithfully, as you would a second job--even if you've already worked an eight-hour shift, or taught four composition classes, or cared for your young children all day. You are never not writing. You think constantly in terms of narrative and sentences, so that after weeks, sometimes years, of waiting and working you will be able to tell a human story as well as you can. If you choose writing as your vocation, these rare, graceful moments will sustain you as well as any unexpected gift, like a warm winter coat, a sturdy table, a small, blue suitcase.

About Grace

"No one can live without memories."–Isabel Allende, *Paula*

I ONCE HEARD THAT DAUGHTERS know more about the maternal side of their families because their mothers and grandmothers record the names of their own ancestors on the front pages of the family Bible, passing it down through the women in the family. I always believed I knew more about my mother's Sicilian ancestry simply because her side of the family was so much larger, and louder, than my father's quiet German relatives. My maternal great-grandparents, Guiseppa and Guiseppe Macaluso, courted on the boat from Palermo and married when they arrived in America in 1904. The story about how they came over on the boat and raised twenty-one children in a cold water flat in the Italian tenements, in the river bottoms of Cincinnati, was a family legend often repeated by my mother.

She recalled Guiseppe at the age of 103, toothless, chewing hard candy with razor sharp gums, drinking a glass of whiskey every day until he died. He'd served in the Italian military before emigrating, and claimed he once met Garibaldi. While stationed in Italy, he also believed serpents dwelled beneath the Straits of Messina. The serpents, he said, were the main reason he and his family never returned to Sicily.

My great-grandmother, Guiseppa, came from a different ilk, a family that historians now call "birds of passage." Temporary migrants forced to fill jobs beneath native-born laborers, they hated America. In the middle of early twentieth century diasporas, when over two-thirds of Sicily's inhabitants fled the island, they traveled back and forth to Palermo like migratory birds, looking for work, ultimately choosing old-world privations over the demoralized conditions they found in the new world. They left my great grandmother behind in Ohio with the husband she met on the boat. By all accounts, she was a happy woman, an avid poker player who carried a deck of cards around in her apron pocket.

23

After a day of simmering sauces and feeding children, she cleared her kitchen table of babies and dishes, and dealt out a hand of five-card draw to anyone willing to sit across from her.

Most of my own family memories are tied to poker games, my grandfather and his brothers playing penny ante at somebody's kitchen table, drinking wine from water glasses, smoking cigars. Dusky-skinned men with heavy accents, they never spoke Italian to anyone but to each other, or their parents. They never told stories about their parents' lives in Sicily or their own early lives in the river bottoms. When asked anything about themselves, they shrugged or told only what happened after they were adults. I don't know all the reasons these men were so reticent about their pasts. Perhaps because they were raised by parents who emigrated from an island defined by loss and silence, they became stoics who never lingered over stories of heritage and upbringing. They were joke-tellers more concerned with assuring their safe passage into the American dream. When I asked my grandfather about his life before meeting my American grandmother, he'd take me on his knee, and speak suddenly in dialect, "C'era una volta, una volta, una volta." He never taught me a word of Italian, so I always assumed he was saying, "I don't wanna. I don't wanna. I don't wanna." I've since learned that this phrase means, "Once upon a time."

Growing up in Ohio, I listened to my mother tell family stories that all could have begun with the phrase "Once upon a time." These stories were more true than fiction, but I wouldn't bet on any of them. My favorite is about how my grandfather met my grandmother. He'd moved out of his parents' flat at fifteen and into a Catholic rectory to work as a hired hand, planning to become a priest. For three years, he lived with priests who made him deliver bottles of bootleg liquor to them in shoeboxes, forcing him to sneak women in through the back door. My grandfather was disillusioned with the priesthood by the time he first saw my grandmother, Joy Sypher.

He'd taken a second job delivering fruit from the river bottoms to Winton Place, the uptown neighborhood where she lived. Next to the grocery market he delivered to, there was an ice cream shop called Greeks, and that was where he first saw my grandmother. A rheumatic invalid's daughter who'd been pulled out of school at the age of eleven to take care of her mother, she was already in her mid twenties, ten years older than my grandfather. Though living in a time of flapper frocks and bobbed hair, she wore a Gibson girl and wove her long blond hair into a braid that reached her waist. Still, when my grandfather saw her blue eyes and blond hair, he saw a real American lady. Taken with her and the "uptown life" of her family in Winton Place, he hatched a plan to impress her. He and his best friend, Ray Perez, dressed up in white cotton trousers and tams, and acquired riding crops. Then they returned to the ice cream parlor where my grandmother was sitting with her cousin, Grace. They introduced themselves as Latin American polo players on their way down to Kentucky horse country. Daughter of two staunch Methodists, my shy grandmother excused herself from these two Catholic boys to go to the restroom. Once there, she jumped out the window, and ran home.

My grandmother never spoke to my mother or me about her early life as an invalid's daughter in Winton Place. These stories all came from Grace. Though she was really my mother's first cousin, my mother called her Aunt Grace because she and my grandmother had grown up like sisters. Grace's mother had divorced the year Grace was born, and she raised Grace with the help of her own mother in another tenement in the German blue shirt district of the river bottoms, near the breweries and her job as a stenographer at a baseball factory called Goldsmiths. Winters, when gas was low and it was too cold to live in their apartment, Grace's mother and grandmother packed up their belongings, and went to live with my great-grandparents in Winton Place. There, Grace's mother kept house for my grandmother's family to earn her keep until it was warm enough to move back down to the river bottoms.

I met Grace in person only once, when I was a child, and I still saw her as she'd been the last time I'd seen her-- in her late sixties, her hair dyed red, styled into a Marcel wave. She wore a bright pink pantsuit, and a slash of vermillion lipstick. By the time Grace began telling me stories about my grandmother, she was ninety-three and blinded by macular degeneration, her breathing labored by a congestive heart condition. She lived alone in Miami, Florida, in the house she'd shared with her deceased husband, Droggy, a Bulgarian immigrant who sometimes came back from the dead to speak to her. I asked Grace what she and Droggy talked about when he returned to her, and she said, "Well, a lot of times I'll be sitting at my vanity. He'll stand behind me while I'm looking in the mirror, and say, "'Red, you got your lipstick on crooked again.'" Another time, Grace informed me that my deceased grand-parents, whom she called Jimmy and Joy, had visited her in Florida. They'd come to invite her to a Saturday night poker game, but Grace told them the timing was bad. She believed staunchly in visitations from the dead, and sometimes delved into who she might have been in her own former life. For this, she visited a gypsy hypnotist who regressed her into memories from her last incarnation. The gypsy tape-recorded Grace speaking in a foreign language while she was under, and for a brief time she harbored hopes of being from foreign aristocracy. Then she had the tape of her hypnotism translated, and discovered she'd been a Ukrainian tenant farmer.

Whatever misgivings I might have had about Grace's ability to converse with the dead, and that foray into her previous incarnation, were diminished by her supple storytelling, her ease with the liminal space she inhabited—somewhere between the living and the dead. She knew what I had yet to learn: we all regress into our former selves in memory, recycling the same people in our lives, especially if things are unresolved. According to my mother, Grace's only daughter had been an alcoholic with lung cancer and a tracheotomy who'd died several years before from pouring too much vodka through the feeding tube in her stomach. As Grace bided her last months "above the sod," as she called it, she worked hard to tidy up the narratives of her life. She commissioned her only-living son, Constance, to rebind her family's Bible that held in its front pages all the records of our ancestors—where they were born, who they married, who died. As Grace poured over her family's mended Bible, she began sending me a series of audio-taped family stories, sharing detailed recollections she called "stuff you never knew about your grandmother," beginning with how my grandmother lived as an invalid's daughter in Winton Place.

The first tape dropped through my mail slot the summer I moved with my husband, Rick, and our toddler son into our first real home, a 1924 bungalow in the historic district of the Carolina mill town where he and I taught writing at a local liberal arts college.

"The story that came down to me was that your great grandmother had rheumatism and arthritis," Grace began in her first tape. "Her hands became twisted, like arthritic people do, and she just sat for the rest of her life. Joy never saw her mother stand or move. She was born after her mother was in this condition, and as soon as she was old enough, probably eleven or twelve, she must have dropped out of school to take over the care of her mother. Every morning, she had to get her mother out of bed, bathe her thoroughly, dress her in lovely clothes, do her hair up on top of her head, and put her on the rocker. They had a set of wheels that went under the rocker that you tilted the rocker back on, and Joy rolled her out into the dining room, and there she would sit all day in front of her desk, and in front of the bay window that overlooked the rock garden that Uncle Bill tended when he wasn't working for the B&O Railroad. When I think back on it, I guess it wasn't much of a life."

Surely, this late in her life, Grace must have felt an urgent need to pass on these memories to someone who'd safe keep them, but her easy-going voice never felt insistent. The tapes arrived at a steady pace. Every month or so, one dropped through the mail slot of my bungalow. Side A of each tape contained another installment of "stuff you never knew about your grandmother," stories about how my grandmother couldn't possibly marry an Italian Catholic boy; how my grandfather, "Jimmy," became a teetotaler and a Methodist so that my grandmother would finally marry him; how my newly-married grandmother became an excellent poker player and teller of jokes so dirty she could make all the men in the family blush; how they all got through the Depression by living in the house up in Winton Place, with my great-grandfather, her Uncle Bill.

On Side B of each tape, Grace recorded an appendix of sorts, a numbered list of random recollections Grace claimed might be of use to me some day. "Number one," she said. " I loved olives." Following this detail, Grace recounted how every Christmas my great grandmother gave her a bottle of olives. She'd put them on the attic stairway because it was cool there, and the olives would keep better. So that Grace wouldn't eat the entire bottle at once, she was allowed to eat one olive every fifteen minutes. Every year, for every Christmas of her childhood, Grace sat on the top attic stair, watching the clock, hollering, "It's time for another olive," every fifteen minutes.

In her memoir, "Sketches of the Past," Virginia Woolf identifies these ordinary and unbidden memories as "moments of being." Woolf believed that narrative is encoded in everyday objects and places from our childhood and early years. Woolf theorized that every storyteller must learn how to identify metaphor in these moments. Once identified, these moments are followed by the desire to explain, first by writing about the experience of the younger self, then by examining the experience through the perspective of the older self. The present rests upon the past, and the past relies upon the present self for interpreting, evaluating, finding meaning behind these single moments of experience that the past self could not understand.

Though Grace never mentioned Virginia Woolf to me, it seems to me now that with each tape Grace infused her stories about my quiet, enigmatic grandmother with details from her own early life. She continually filtered the past through her present consciousness, probed the most ordinary details for meaning. Her narrative line skipped backward and forward, as memory does. Though she often speculated, "I think that was true" and "This was how it must have been," she wove historical awareness into her personal memories. Her Great Depression stories were grounded by details about World War I soldiers selling apples on the street corners for five cents a piece; her World War II stories were peppered with draft board reports.

In her memoir, Woolf writes that memories are the base that life stands upon, that life is a "bowl that one fills and fills and fills." The summer Grace's tapes began arriving, I walked in a fever dream of young motherhood, trying to hold onto my past self as an aspiring writer by reading Hugo, Flaubert, and Dostoevsky while my toddler son slept. I often felt dim, empty-headed from heat and sleeplessness, unable to hold a single printed word in my mind. Books fell out of my hands as I drifted off to sleep in the middle of a sentence, and I'd awake with a red crease on my forehead where the binding of Madame Bovary had landed. In this bovine state, I played Grace's tapes over and over again, filling myself with her stories, absorbing their cadences. I drifted off to them and awoke at different places in time, feeling pleasantly disoriented, unworried about whether I were in the past or present.

Since my own earliest memories, my mother drilled into me the idea that when a woman receives a gift in a serving bowl, she should never return that bowl empty. As Grace delivered platter upon platter of voluptuous stories to me, it seemed rude to respond to her with an empty bowl of silence. I had no great stories of my own, but I lived in a storied house, on a street shaded by dogwoods and ancient magnolias, lined by grand dame Victorians and bungalows that once belonged to the local dairy farm owners whose wives wanted "town houses." Many of my neighbors were widows from other parts of the South—Tidewater, Virginia, New Orleans, Mobile, Alabama—women who migrated to South Carolina with husbands, and lived on in the historic homes after their husbands' deaths, tending each other, and their gardens.

I decided to carry my tape recorder through each room of my bungalow, describing for Grace its 12-foot ceilings, its heart pine window seats, the coal fireplaces with black screens before them, how every room radiated from the dining room at the center of the house. I saved the description of my favorite room, the master bedroom, for last. Its west-facing window was shaded by overhangs, and an ancient spoon magnolia served as a screen between our window and the neighboring house. The room's navy wallpaper swirled with pink magnolia blossoms. In the spring, the magnolias in the wallpaper framed the living spoon magnolia blooming outside the window, frail sunlight filtering through its leaves. The room remained a mystical blue all day long, good for sleeping on the thick brass bed I'd found disassembled at an auction, its head and foot rails so thickly patinaed that nobody saw its value. I bought it for ten dollars, soaked, polished and reassembled its parts until it was bright and sturdy again. It filled the entire bedroom, and I felt pleased by how solidly beautiful this bed was, by how I managed to spy its value beneath an ancient coat of green. I believed it kept my back when I sat my writing desk tucked into the corner of the bedroom, just inside the doorway.

Grace responded to my tape with a description of my grandmother's house, the bungalow in Winton Place. "The description of your house was charming," she said. "It got me thinking about the house. It had high ceilings, and sliding glass doors and big bay windows. It had a dining room with a table that would have sat twelve people, and after Aunt Emma died, everything got a little looser and a little easier to live in the house. Joy and Jimmy were living in it with Uncle Bill. She used to give quite a few parties, and we played a lot of penny ante poker. We figured if you couldn't lose more than a few pennies that was all right. I remember one time Uncle Bill found a gilt picture frame, put it on an easel, and glued on an entire deck of cards. One of the games we played when Joy had a party was to throw darts at the cards, and we played poker that way, throwing darts at the cards to see if we could get a pair, three of a kind, straight, full house. We got pretty good at it. But Uncle Bill never threw anything away. He could always find a use for something. You would have liked him. He was big and kind of silent and smiled slowly. I don't remember him ever laughing out loud, but he had a long, slow smile that just kind of blossomed."

Curiously, whenever Grace mailed a tape to me, she also called my mother in order to tell her stories of a slightly different nature. My mother called me from Ohio every Sunday at 10 a.m. Always, the weekend after Grace sent a tape to me, my mother called a few minutes early. Mortified by another one of my grandmother's secrets that Grace had spilled over the phone to her, my mother recounted the grittier, more realistic details Graced had left out of the tapes.

"Grace called again," my mom began. "She said my mother wasn't pretty. Then she started telling me about how my mother had some pregnancy scare with a grocery boy when she was seventeen. Who wants to hear such stories about her own mother?"

Well, I surely wanted to hear such stories, mainly because they took the fairy-tale edge off the stories Grace was giving me, adding another dimension. Though my mother didn't want to hear the darker secrets about her mother, she certainly wanted to tell them. After every phone call to my mother, Grace would send another tape to me, including an indirect apologia for the darker details she'd given my mother over the phone, a slight amendment to the stories she'd told me in the previous tape: "I think I hurt your mother's feelings the other night when I said that Joy was never very pretty," Grace said. "I guess we just didn't think of her that way because she looked so old fashioned. Aunt Emma kept her looking like a little spinster. Her shoes were different, her socks were dark, her clothes were very plain. She wore little flat hats. Her hair was in a braid—she had beautiful hair, beautiful eyes, full lips. I think she must have dropped out of high school. I have no idea how far in school she went, but her life was devoted to taking care of her mother. They would get cleaning help and stuff like that, and Aunt Emma would order groceries over the phone, and they would be delivered, which gave Joy the first opportunity to know about boys. The grocery delivery boy was the first man she ever dated, and she went with him quite a while. I can't remember his name. She was very much in love with him, and she was very broken up when it all ended."

Along with this tape, Grace included a picture of my grandmother that reaffirmed her old-fashioned beauty and innocence. She's sixteen or seventeen, around the time she must have been going with the delivery boy. Dressed in a Gibson Girl, she sits on a milking stool wearing black lace-up shoes, and her blond braid winds down to her waist like a bull whip. She smiles softly, a faraway look in her eyes.

Back and forth, the stories flew from Grace to me, from Grace to my mother, from my mother back to me, the two of them going over our family history, constantly revising, filling in more and more back story, amending, always speculating, "I think this was true" and "This was how it must have been."

Between the times when Grace's tapes arrived, I mothered, taught, and tried to write my own stories. In clement weather, I went outside to chat with my favorite neighbor, Meg, an 83-year-old retired librarian who hailed from a tiny town outside of Mobile, Alabama, that had disappeared. Like Grace, Meg suffered from an ocular disease, and lived alone. I came to know her through conversations we held over the fence that separated my yard from her garden. A tiny woman with a halo of short, thinning curls, Meg gardened in a man's white t-shirt and calf-length pajama bottoms. On early summer mornings, before the day's heat and bugs took over, I'd find Meg sitting cross-legged among waist-high purple bearded iris, hedging the bed with empty wine bottles transients threw in the ravine behind our houses as they passed through the neighborhood. A practitioner of poverty economics, Meg traded fragrant lily bulbs for antique roses the other widows dug up and carried from their own hometowns. She never watered anything she put in the ground. She believed in the providence of rain. If it didn't rain the flowers weren't meant to live, so her garden died out a bit every August.

Once, I tried to surprise Meg with a painted pot for her garden. I asked her favorite color. She must have thought I was giving her an item of clothing because she said flatly, "I'm past all that." Slowly, over the garden fence, I learned pieces of everything that she was past. I learned how her family had paved their drive and garden paths with oyster shells every summer. I learned what it was like to grow up the only daughter of a woman who favored sons. Whenever Meg acted in a way her mother believed unseemly her mother "sent her to Coventry," which was a soft phrase for a hard silent treatment her mother gave her for days, sometimes weeks. Like my grandmother and Grace, Meg had escaped a mortifying childhood home by marrying. Unlike the women in my family, she'd married her hometown sweetheart, who became an astrophysics professor at Yale, where she found a job working as a college librarian. There had been a beloved child, a daughter who died at seven of leukemia. The husband planted a Japanese maple in their front yard to memorialize the child. Then, he left her.

Meg's only remark about this subject was, "He couldn't live with the grief anymore. He said he just wanted to marry a moneyed woman who would take care of him." Three husbands followed, and she had a daughter with each one, but Meg rarely mentioned the other husbands except to call them "the children's fathers." It was the first husband, the sweetheart from the vanished hometown, who returned to her every August for a week-long visit.

I always knew when the ex-husband was coming because something lavish appeared in Meg's garden. Typically, the week before the ex-husband arrived, Meg took off in her Kia Rio to a local nursery, the fancy one that sold expensive garden elements--solar northern light spheres, or cerulean-blue bottle trees with trendy names like "Seagrass," or "The Haint Chaser." The summer I learned of Meg's reunions with her ex-husband, she returned with a copper sprinkler shaped like a butterfly surrounded by spinning rings. She mounted this sprinkler system in a sun-bleached paddling pool shaped like a turtle, and attached it to her hose. When she turned it on, it spun like a spherical astrolabe as she kept time with her ex husband on the sun porch screened by an ancient camellia that fanned across the entire back of her house. When I glimpsed Meg and her ex-husband sitting side by side on the sun porch, heads bent together, drinking tea and talking, I turned away, feeling as if I'd witnessed a most intimate moment. At the same time, I wondered what those two must have talked about all week long. How had they overcome the early sorrow of their marriage, and arrived at this summer arrangement so late in life?

Grace's final tape arrived in January, the stories ending with my great-grandfather's death. The week after Christmas in 1939 was my grandmother's birthday, and my grandparents were planning to go to a dance downtown. Joy, my grandmother, went out to buy a dress, and Jimmy, my grandfather, was at work. Uncle Bill called Jimmy at work to ask what he wanted for dinner, and gave him a choice. Jimmy chose sausage. So Uncle Bill walked down to the grocery store at the foot of the hill and bought the sausage. He came back up, put it in a pan, and dropped dead in the kitchen. That's where Jimmy found him when he came home.

On Side B, the appendix listed only one detail, a single moment Grace seemed not to understand: "The only thing I remember about Uncle Bill's funeral was standing at the bier, looking at him and saying to myself, 'I never realized he had such huge ears. They were so long.' That's kind of a stupid thing to remember about my uncle, whom I loved so much."

After her father's death, my grandmother sold the house and everything in it. She turned everything she could into cash. According to Grace, the dining room had a plate rail around it, where the family sat pretty dishes about three feet from the ceiling. People gave my grandmother beautiful hand-painted plates, all china. "They were all gone," Grace said. "They disappeared. And all Joy said was, 'You can get a lot of money out of the silverware.' All she could remember about that house was work and anybody who died was always laid out in the corner of the living room. All she wanted to do was get rid of the memories. I think that's true. I loved that house, but she hated it."

Like Grace, I'd come to love my grandmother's house and the memories it held. When Grace's tapes stopped arriving, I felt the loss that comes at the end of every good story. I typed up all the stories and sent a copy of the transcriptions to my mother, who copied and distributed them among her cousins, and to Grace's son, Constance. I kept the original tapes, and listened to them over and over again. I filled up on those stories until they became my own.

Around this time, Meg had a car accident. It was during our yearly ice storm, when the ancient oaks and pines that leaned over our houses cracked beneath the thin coat of ice that coated their limbs and trunks. A pine fell on our power lines, cutting off our electricity. The city didn't salt or clear the roads, so the ice froze, melted, and refroze for days after the storm. Meg went out for supplies, and another driver t-boned her Kia. The car was irreparable, and her insurance company refused to pay. By the time she got her car fixed, January had melted into late February, a time of chill rain and colorless skies. The only promise of spring in our muddy yards resided in the ancient camellias blooming at the back of our houses. My camellia was shooting off bright magenta blooms. Meg's flamed with coral blossoms.

I was standing at the window, admiring Meg's camellia, when a formal invitation for a tea party at her house dropped through my mail slot. At first the invitation confused me. Meg and I rarely saw the inside of each other's homes; our friendship formed outside, over a garden fence, in spring, summer, and early fall. Before this invitation, I'd never envisioned what Meg did inside her house during winter months. I'd also never been to a formal Southern tea party before. After a week of deliberation, I carried a pecan pie and Grace's tapes over to Meg's house. I knocked on her front door, rather than taking the back garden path that led to her sun porch. I recall standing there for a long time.

Waiting for Meg to answer the door, I studied the curious planter she'd made out of an old exercise bike. She'd placed pots filled with spider ivy in a basket that hung from the handlebars. The winter-pale leaves cascaded over the pedals and seat.

When Meg finally answered, she wore a floral tea dress with a coral camellia blossom pinned in her hair. The inside of her house was small and dimly lit, its front room filled with furnishings she must have rescued from her previous marriages—a single china plate displayed on the fireplace mantle; a green velvet loveseat and chairs with crocheted lace antimacassars on their backs; a Persian rug that had faded to the color of a faun, its patterns barely distinguishable. In the middle of the front room, she'd set a table with a white linen tablecloth and napkins. She'd floated more camellia blooms in fine china bowls between two tapered candles. Though I was the only guest, the table was solid with food. Ham, pineapple, and cucumber sandwiches with the crusts cut off were piled on a three-tiered stand made out of candlesticks and mismatched china plates. Finger bowls were mounded with olives, almonds, and cheese wafers with pecan halves pressed into their centers. Beside a basket of fluffy tea biscuits, salt spoons were dipped into tiny jars of apricot, blueberry, and hot pepper jelly. The table was set with mismatched plates and cups, and a silver tea service was filled with black and green teas.

Over tea, I learned that the car accident had shaken Meg so badly that she couldn't bring herself to drive. She hadn't left her house for all of January, not even to go out for groceries. Homebound, she'd tried Mobile Meals, but became mortified when the first volunteer made her pray before eating. Meg's serious soul work took place during those quiet mornings in her garden, but when the Jehovah's Witnesses patrolled our neighborhood, she invited them onto her sun porch for iced tea. They didn't count their afternoons with Meg as part of their witnessing. She considered them friends.

"Not even the Jehovah's Witnesses make me pray like that," she said.

About this time, I realized that my company was a commodity worth what must have been her first foray out of the house for groceries since the accident. Honored by the pains she'd taken for this party, I felt moved by the dignified way she'd chosen to quell her fear and isolation. I played Grace's tapes for her, and after the tapes were over I showed her the picture of my grandmother. Meg identified my grandmother's Gibson girl and black lace-up boots, placing them around 1900s, verifying that my grandmother had indeed been dressed twenty years behind the styles of her time. But she seemed more interested in the details about Grace's mother, how she rented rooms to the men who worked in the breweries to supplement her salary at the baseball factory, how she took a breast pump to work with her at the baseball factory, secretly pumping during her breaks so that she could feed her daughter, and still keep her job.

After we finished with the tapes and photographs, Meg led me back to the butler's pantry, a space between her kitchen and the sun porch that held a desk and a computer. Lit by winter light coming from the sun porch, the space was cluttered with old news clippings. It smelled of dust and loneliness. Meg turned on her computer, and began showing me pictures and news clips about her hometown, and the people who once belonged to it.

Though her records were organized with a librarian's diligence, there seemed to be nothing whole remaining of her hometown, or its people. She'd filled an entire hard drive with pictures of scattered bricks, old lumber, roads paved with crushed oyster shells, lone chimneys crawling with vines. There were street signs, the remains of cellars, and wells. She kept one picture framed on top of the computer. Mounted on cardboard gilded at the edges, it was of a glamorous young woman, petite and dusky skinned, her full lips slashed with dark vermillion, a stray curl of raven hair blowing across her forehead. She knelt on a swath of grass beside a pram, her eyes gazing softly at a toddler who strayed just beyond her reach.

I studied the photo, startled by the young woman's beauty, until I realized that this was Meg, before she was "past it." I also realized what was not in the picture—the man who took the shot, a husband still besotted with his wife and child.

"Did your first husband take this?"

Meg nodded. "He was an armchair photographer."

"You were so beautiful," I marveled.

"I kept my looks for a long time," she said.

I stared at the photograph, amazed by her beauty, and by the gaping loss that fueled her search for the bits and pieces remaining from her home and history. I began to understand how she overcame the indignity of her ex-husband's abandonment during the depths of her life's biggest sorrow. I could see why she welcomed him back once a year, now that they were old. The husband wasn't just her first sweetheart. He was her home, the time and place upon which all her other memories rested. I recalled Grace's latest efforts to arrange our own family history, and send it all to me for safekeeping. I thought about how memories-- even the secret, mortifying ones--link us back to our truest selves, and sustain us as we grow older. None of us could afford to get past them.

One Sunday in April my mother called three hours before her regular time. I was in bed, lying half asleep, half awake.

"Grace died." Her voice was breathless, full of an urgency to tell. I waited for her to fill me in on the details of Grace's final days in the hospital. "She lived there for a full week, but when she died, all of her nurses were surprised to find out that she was blind."

"How do you suppose that happened?" I said. "Didn't they look at her chart?"

"Maybe they missed it."

"Maybe she told them so many stories they forgot that she couldn't see."

We paused, and in the solemn silence I looked outside the bedroom window. Pine pollen had fallen over the magnolia. Its limbs were powdered by the fluorescent green dust that would keep falling over this part of South Carolina for a solid week. It would drift thickly across car windshields, blurring my vision of the pink dogwoods beside my house, the purple bearded iris that crowded my flowerbeds. Soon the air and earth around me would become one flurry of green, pinks, purples, and reds. As my mother filled me in on the less dignified details of Grace's dying-- the tired heart no longer pumping, the fluid-filled lungs, the kidney failure--I closed my eyes and imagined her in a pink flowered hospital gown that surely she would have talked a nurse into giving her. I saw her sitting straight up in her hospital bed, applying her bright red lipstick, her beloved husband's hand guiding her hand so that she could keep her lipstick on straight. I imagined my grandparents visiting, inviting her to poker night, Grace finally accepting their offer. She may have been blind, but she never stopped seeing. She must have known that the timing was finally right.

"What are you doing?" my mother asked.

"I was just lying here with my eyes closed," I said.

"Well, I suppose Grace had a secret of her own," my mother said.

My mother and I continued talking, collaborating on the known and unknown details of Grace's final days in the hospital until we came up with the story that was exactly how it must have been. Outside my window, the pink magnolia blossoms opened like teacups, filling and filling with the fine dust of pines.

The Peach Season

"There were ten thousand thousand fruit to touch,
Cherish in hand, lifted down, and not let fall"
—Robert Frost, "After Apple Picking"

IN THE FOURTH YEAR OF OUR MARRIAGE, my husband, Rick, and I took jobs teaching college English in a South Carolina mill town in the middle of peach country. Our first summer there, on a Saturday in mid-July, we had exactly five dollars in our checking account, a tank of gas, and a one-year-old baby who only took naps in his car seat while the motor ran. We took a drive with no destination in mind, only the desire to lull our son, Hunter, to sleep. We headed east on Main Street, toward Cowpens, a pasturing town that grew up around a Revolutionary War site. There, murals of redcoats marched along the sides of the antique shop, greeting us as we passed through the town.

Beyond the turn off for the battlefield, we crossed the interstate and under a trestle just as a freight train bearing peaches rolled above us. We slowed as we reached a field of trees whose limbs opened like rows of green vases in pastures that sloped for miles on both sides of the road. The trees were heavy with blushing peaches. We rolled down the windows, letting the heady scent fill the car. When we reached a roadside produce market and peach packing warehouse, we parked beside a white picket fence below a sign that announced "The Sweetest Peaches Anywhere, U- Pick, We Pick, $10 a bushel."

The owner of the orchards, Mr. Cash, was running the stand that day, selling baskets of peaches, ciders, jams, and cobbler mixes. A middle-aged man in a cowboy hat, he stood behind a freezer case, scooping out cones of home-churned ice cream for a couple of disoriented travelers, giving them directions back to the highway while ringing up their purchases. When it was our turn, we asked Mr. Cash if we could buy a half bushel, and said we'd like to pick our own. We'd brought nothing to put the peaches in, so he let us borrow an empty bushel basket, saying, "You can use this one as long as you promise to return it when you're done."

He began chatting us up, explaining that he grew a series of orchards that ripened in overlapping windows through eighteen weeks of summer. It had been a good peach season for him. The foothills of Cherokee County had protected the blossoms from late spring frosts, and there had been plenty of water at this elevation. He said a local couple had decided to get married in his orchards in April, celebrating their nuptials among bows laden with pink petals. "When you have a good season, every day's like a wedding this time of year," he said.

He directed us to an orchard we hadn't seen from the main road, where a variety of mid-season peaches called Red Globes glowed from within the green shaggy branches. We drove up a winding dirt road, and parked beside a barn and corral where a bay horse loitered in the pasture beside a concrete water trough. Standing outside the car, I was tempted to stop at the field's edge, where the trees staggered beneath the weight of peaches, but I feared we might miss the sweetest ones if we didn't move deeper into the center of the orchard, where the trees bowed over the paths, dropping fruit.

Hunter looked drowsy, so we put him in his stroller where he'd have some shade, and rolled him into the orchard. Rick picked a peach, took a bite, handing it to me. I lifted it up. It did resemble a tiny red globe, an entire planet alive and warm in my palm. I took a bite. The furry skin broke, the tart yellow flesh splashed across my tongue, and the juices ran down my chin, arms, and elbows. I gave Hunter a bite. His feet bounced, and he grabbed for it. The noon sun pleasantly pounded my shoulders through my t-shirt, and Hunter fell asleep, finally, to the rhythm of falling peaches.

The ripest ones were fermenting on the branches in the mid-day sun, liquifying into a noon wine so heady that I caught a contact high that sent me scrambling through the pathways, oblivious to the field heat and the peaches squashing beneath my feet. I began searching for the perfect ones, the kind with a yellow hue running just beneath their ruby skin. They needed to be sweet and tart, but not too tart, softer

40

than a tennis ball, but not too soft. There could be no nicks, bruises, or scratches. Above all, they had to smell exactly like a peach must taste— sweet and tangy, alive on the tongue. Mindful that we had to hold ourselves down to a half bushel, I began picking exactly one peach off each tree in the orchard.

I picked off high and low branches, and once I picked one off the ground. It split open in my hand, and I saw a bee swimming drunkenly in the juices around the pit, happily drowning. I set that one gently at the base of the tree, continuing on.

The orchard was so full of ripe peaches, and so empty of pickers, that there was no hope of anyone harvesting them all before they fell. Occasionally, I'd sneak a taste of one-- just to be sure I was selecting the best. I held it up, examining its flawless blush. If sweetness were a color, it would be this shade of peach, I thought. I walked over to Rick, and urged him to taste it. He took a bite. A slow smile bloomed across his face. He deposited our sleeping son and his stroller in the shade, and began picking alongside me. We buzzed from tree to tree, picking and sampling the irresistible fruit as our son slept in a swoon.

Our bushel half full, we pushed Hunter's stroller back toward the horse barn. We reached a tree that must have been split by lightning, half its bent trunk forming a makeshift bench to rest upon. There, we sat examining two bright peaches growing from within its bare branches, marveling at how something so alive could be growing out of something so dead. The bored horse became curious about us, and he wandered over to the fence. Hunter awoke, his brown eyes wide, as if he were aware of the little peach-picking party Rick and I'd been having without him while he slept. We walked him over to the fence to see the horse. I picked a peach off the ground, held it out in my palm for the horse. He took it whole, rolling it thoughtfully around his mouth, sorting flesh from seed with his teeth, then spitting the pit out clean. Hunter belly laughed as if this were a party trick.

When we stopped feeding him, the horse ran back to the middle of the pasture, rearing up, dancing around the water trough. We took the bushel basket back to the produce market. Mr. Cash poured the peaches into paper bags without weighing them as we wrote out a check for our last five dollars. He chucked Hunter under the chin, said, "Why she is the prettiest baby I've ever seen," and in that moment my son did look pretty, his brown eyes wide, his mahogany hair curling gently around his heat-flushed cheeks. The question of his gender seemed petty compared to this man's generosity. I opted not to correct him. He swept Hunter into his arms and put him in the basket we'd just emptied, carrying him around the stand like a bushel of ripe fruit. Then, he gave him a cup of peach ice cream. We fished out some quarters to pay him, but he waved our money away. At the picnic table outside the market, we sampled spoonfuls of the ice cream as we took turns feeding it to our son.

At home, I discovered the obvious, that we'd picked too many peaches for our small family to eat before they spoiled. I spent the next hour delivering peaches to neighbors--the librarian from Alabama next door, the artist from Virginia up the street, the schoolteacher from New Orleans two streets over. Finished with my goodwill mission, I returned to the house and broke out my grandmother's peach cobbler recipe. Rick turned on a little Louis Armstrong, Hunter's favorite. He was wide awake after sleeping most of the afternoon, ready to be held. I rigged our convertible baby carrier to my back, and Rick lifted him into it. In this way, I peeled and sliced peaches into a shallow dish, sprinkling the slices with cinnamon. I worked butter into flour and sugar, dropping large spoonfuls of this mixture on top of the peaches before sliding them into the oven. As the cobbler cooked, I swayed and danced Hunter around the kitchen to Louis Armstrong tunes, feeling his deep belly laugh against my back, his feet bouncing to the cadence of "Cake Walkin' Babies," "A Fine Romance."

I must have had this romance with peaches in mind the late-summer day after we returned from dropping Hunter off for his first year of college in Nashville, where he'd been accepted into the music school, and would begin preparing for a career as a professional bassist. Home from Tennessee, I stood in his room. A Gibson Les Paul Standard and Viola Epiphone were propped up in opposite corners. Steinbeck's *The Pearl* was cracked open on his desk. Tolkien, Huxley, and Orwell had been tucked between the sideboards and mattress of his bed.

I felt at once proud and guilty, remembering the white lie I'd told Hunter to keep him reading good books through his teenage years, that the greatest musicians and songwriters in modern history had all aspired to be English teachers in their earlier lives, and were well-schooled in the classics. Now, I realized that my son had been lulling himself asleep by reading these books, memorizing their cadences, filling his head with their printed words with hopes of transforming their rhythms into music.

Standing among the detritus of all he'd taken with him, I had the overwhelming urge to spend the morning filling a basket with peaches, the afternoon cutting butter into flour, kneading dough delicately into pie pans. I wanted to mix peach slices with sugar, pour and tuck this mixture under another layer of dough, baking it until the peaches liquefied, bubbling out of the crust's corners. I wanted to serve this pie up with ice cream that was custard-based and studded with peaches, like the kind I remembered eating at Mr. Cash's produce market.

I took off in my truck, heading east toward the orchards. As I passed through Cowpens, I slowed, startled by the transformation of the Revolutionary War murals on the side of the antique store. Had the soldiers' coats always been blue instead of red? Had they always aimed their muskets directly at the street traffic? The town had grown since I'd last been there. The Main Street was lined with a new French bakery and a couple of boutiques. The antique store had expanded into a gallery with a bright, blue door. Distracted by all the new businesses, I forgot where the turn-off for the Cash peach orchards had been. I parked in front of the antique store, and walked inside to ask for directions.

Inside the store, I wandered through a carefully arranged clutter of new and old. Bath soaps and organic candles sat on top of antique vanities; Depression-glass vases sprouted among trendy water fountains shaped like lily pads. Earlier that summer, the whole town had celebrated the Mighty Moo Festival, a yearly event honoring the crewmen of the USS Cowpens, veterans of WWII who returned every year for a parade, beauty pageant, and a golf tournament. The antique gallery remained strung with wilted red, white and blue streamers. Leftover

Mighty Moo Festival t-shirts were stacked neatly on shelves within the open doors of a refurbished armoire.

I walked up to the cash register and asked the owner for directions to the turn-off for the Cash Farms.

"I thought I'd go out and pick some peaches," I said.

The storeowner's eyes dropped, and the celebratory air drained swiftly from the store. The wilted streamers beside the cash register seemed to sag a bit lower.

"I don't think there's anybody out there," the storekeeper said.

"What do you mean? I used to go out there every–" I stopped. How many seasons had passed since I'd last gone out to pick peaches?

"Hasn't been anyone out there for years," she said.

"So you can't go and pick peaches?"

"Not that I know of."

"Can you still buy the peaches at the stand?"

The woman looked genuinely puzzled. "You can try, but I don't think there's anything out there."

"I think I'll go check it out, see if I can at least buy some peaches."

I felt so bad about casting a mysterious gloom over the festive store that I bought a Mighty Moo t-shirt for my father, a history buff who once enjoyed visiting the battlefield with me years before. The owner smiled as she rang up my purchase. "When you come back through, let me know what you found."

How strange, I thought as I drove over the interstate and neared the place where those lovely orchards had been. Only a few trees remained in the middle of some weedy fields. They reached like arthritic hands from the earth, surrounded by round bales of gray hay. Tall grasses with purple tassels swayed softly between them. The warehouse stood empty, and the faded roadside produce sign out front leaned over the faded and broken picket fence. The darkened windows of the market were filled with "Keep Out" and "No Trespassing" signs.

I drove around to the back of the warehouse, searching for an orchard I might have missed. To the left of the building, there was a small stand of spindly trees guarded by another Keep Out sign. Behind the warehouse, the open loading dock was a graveyard of farming equipment--a row of blossom thinners, mowers and tractors upended beside a lopsided pile of tractor tires. I kept driving, searching for the orchard where we'd picked the Red Globe peaches years before.

The road was straighter than I remembered, and the fields were planted with something low, dark, and burly. Crows rose from a few exhausted stalks of corn, circling their burnt tassels. I found an old spook house with all its windows missing, its front door swung wide open. Though it looked like no one lived there anymore, its front room remained furnished with a cherry wood bedroom suite. From within the fence that surrounded the tiny yard and front porch, a bright bower of pink zinnias, blue coneflowers, and red poppies brimmed. Farther down the road, I saw the horse barn, its tin roof streaked with rust, half of it caved in, the other half rolled back from its rafters. The corral was filled with more high weeds, but empty of that peach-loving horse.

About a half mile down from the abandoned corral, I found an orchard of trees set back from the road, growing in militant rows. Though they were not bearing peaches, their leaves were thick, green and unwilted by the sun, their branches pruned into uniform urns. Beguiled by my own nostalgia, I considered taking a walk along the paths between them. I swerved into a pull-off beside an open metal gate hung with a shooting target shaped like a human silhouette and shot through with hundreds of bullets. The words above it read, "2nd Amendment Security, Nothing Inside Worth Dying For."

As I stared at the bullet-ripped silhouette hanging from the fence, an eerie cloud of common sense drifted into the back of my mind. I decided there was nothing here worth dying for. I got back in my truck, rolled up the window, and locked the doors. I looked up the number for the nearest peach stand on my cell phone.

I located one down the interstate, close to Gaffney, a town in the heart of peach country marked by a 135-foot water tower resembling a giant peach known locally as "The Peachoid." As I passed by, I saw a road crew scrubbing its rosy cleft, overlay stem and leaf with a fire hose and an enormous, long-handled brush. Not far from the Peachoid, I found a frontage-road produce market. A middle-aged woman and her teenage son sat outside the market among the peach bushels, offering samples of a variety called Blaze Prince. The woman handed a sample to me. It was smaller than a Red Globe, its skin a high red color, its flesh almost orange.

"I was just over at the Cash Farms," I said. "They were closed down, and most of the orchards were gone. What happened to them?"

The woman glanced over at her son, and stood, "You'd better follow me inside."

I followed the woman into the store, and she closed the glass door behind her. There among the ciders and jellies, she lowered her voice. "Mr. Cash died a few years ago," she said.

"I'm so sorry," I said.

"The Cherokee County serial killer shot him."

"What?"

My heart began pounding as the woman explained how Mr. Cash had begun selling hay during the leanest years of the Recession, and how the killer had first come to his house under the pretense of buying a bale of hay.

"They say the killer was after the wife, but she'd gone out on some errands when he came back later that day. When she got home, she found her husband shot dead on the living room floor."

Four years had passed, but I still remembered the killer's shooting spree in 2009, the murders of five people in a span of six days. I remembered the attending deputy's public statement after the police shot and killed the murderer: "He was unpredictable. He was scary. He was weird." Strangely, I did not remember that the killer had murdered that sweet farmer, the owner of my beloved peach farm.

"His widow couldn't afford to keep up the orchards after that," the produce lady said. "It was just too much."

This is too much, I thought, numbly watching the produce stand lady pack an extra-large Styrofoam cup with peach ice cream and fill a sack with peaches. I paid her, but I don't remember how much. Outside, the sky was heavy, swirled with white and gunmetal clouds. In the distance, the newly-washed Peachoid gleamed like an obscene red moon above an evergreen windbreak. All the murders had been frightening and tragic, but there was something especially indecent about the killing of that kind peach farmer, the attendant death of so many orchards.

At the house, I told my husband about the murder of the farmer who'd owned the orchards where we'd picked peaches when our son was a baby. Rick nodded sympathetically, and tasted a peach. The interstate peaches had been refrigerated, their ripening stunted before they'd reached their peak. They were a little too hard, and not a single drop of juice ran down my arms. The home-churned ice cream was clotted with chunks of ice. Still shocked by the news of the serial killer, I forgot about making pies, and pulled out the blender. I sliced all the peaches into it, poured in ice, spiced rum and sugar, and pulsed everything together. I served this bright, boozy slush in two parfait glasses, one for Rick and one for me.

We took our drinks out to the back deck, and sat beneath Hunter's bedroom window, from where bass cadences once pulsed on nights when our son, his head full of music, forgot himself and played well past midnight. Though the walls sometimes shook, the house had felt fuller, safer, as if every room had been sheltered by our son's steady rhythms. I'd grown so used to his midnight playing that the sound of his bass often lulled me to sleep. As we sipped our peach cocktails, Rick and I began talking about what our son might be doing in Nashville that very moment, what music he'd been listening to and learning in his college classes all week. When the conversation waned and the air around us became too silent, Rick brought out his Gibson Hummingbird acoustic, plucked a few chords of "Harvest Moon." He only knew part of the song, and when his playing trailed off, he settled the guitar back into its case. I gulped the rest of my makeshift cocktail, listening to the shrill churning of end-of-summer crickets as night fell invisibly around us.

I didn't attempt to buy any peaches for the rest of that summer. I didn't buy fresh peaches the following summer either—until I noticed the sickly grocery store kind that Rick had placed in the fruit bowl in the kitchen. Rick rarely asks me to bring home treats for him, especially ones found at produce stands, so I knew that he, too, harbored some lingering nostalgia for those orchards. We couldn't let another season go by without eating a single fresh peach.

The following morning was a Saturday. I woke early and went down to the local farmers market beside the old train station in search of peaches. The parking lot was larger than the market itself, brimming with mini-vans. I waded through the crowd, lingering at each booth. I took in the briny smell of shrimp and oysters two fishermen had brought up from Shem Creek that morning; the sweet red and poblano peppers displayed like jewels in baskets; the streaky heirloom tomatoes and black mission figs. I tasted every flavor at the pimento cheese dip booth, and moved on to a soy candle vendor. I smelled candles with names like "Kiss Me," "Touch Me," "Sweet Surrender" until I became confused, and they all began to smell like a cross between suntan lotion and a pina colada.

Just beyond the candles, I caught the headier scent of peaches. An elderly farmer stood among baskets brimming with a late-season variety named "Big Red," calling out, "Now that's a stone-free peach, some good eatin'." He sliced one open. "Look at the juice running down my elbows. Look at my smile. We've gotta 18-week season, and we're not done yet."

Tall and slender with white whiskers on his chin, the farmer looked a little bit older than Mr. Cash would have been if he were still alive. As I waited for him to sell peaches to a few couples at five dollars a bag, it occurred to me that I wanted only one peach, a perfect one, to eat out of hand as I browsed the rest of the market. When I finished looking at all the beautiful summer produce at every stand, I would return to buy an entire bag for Rick.

"Could I just buy one peach?" I said.

The farmer nodded as I looked through the baskets above and below the table. The Big Reds were larger than the Red Globes, more fragrant than the Blaze Princes. But I was having trouble deciding which one would be the perfect peach. "I'd like to eat one right now, for breakfast," I explained to the farmer. "Do you see one that looks ready for that?"

The farmer tossed a few peaches around the basket and handed one to me. "Here, try this one," he said. I handed him a five-dollar bill. He pocketed it. I waited for my change as he moved on to help the next customers, exchanging whole bags of peaches for their five-dollar bills.

"I believe I gave you a five-dollar bill," I said. The farmer nodded, his face so impassive that I wasn't sure if he'd heard me. "I only bought one peach."

He nodded again, but didn't move to make change. I waited for a teasing smile, thinking he might be kidding. The smile never came.

"You just charged me five dollars for one peach," I said.

The farmer reached into his pocket and pulled out my five-dollar bill. "You don't think my peach is worth it?" he said.

"That's not the point," I said. "You're charging everyone else five dollars for a whole bag of peaches, and you just charged me five dollars for one."

"If you don't think my peach is worth it, then here's your money." He slapped my five-dollar bill on the table. As I moved to return the peach he stopped my hand. "You can have it for free, if that's all you think it's worth."

I wavered, wondering if the peach was worth it. By this time, I'd expected to be biting through its furry skin, its juices running happily down to my elbows—just as this farmer had promised. As we stood at this bargaining impasse, I stepped aside and walked away from the stand in a daze, the peach awkward and heavy in my hand.

Now, with the luxury of time and distance, I consider the kind of life that might have led this man to charge his mean price. Maybe he'd spent all of spring protecting blossoms from late frosts, and early summer guarding against cankers, cutworms, and moths. Maybe he'd spend the rest of August and September saving late-season varieties from drought. Now I know that the farmer had not killed my memory of a rare moment with my young family in that first orchard, not entirely. Now I believe his bitterness taught me the immeasurable worth of sweetness.

At the time, I simply walked away from the farmer's table and through the rest of the market, my skin prickling with late-summer heat and embarrassment. I stopped at a booth where some women were selling organic chickens. They pulled several plucked and headless chickens out of a giant ice chest, explaining the vegetarian diet they'd fed the chickens while they were alive, the hygienic method they'd used to butcher them. The women's faces were so hopeful and kind that I couldn't tell them that I wasn't in the market for a vegetarian chicken, or that I didn't have enough cash on me to pay ten dollars a pound for one--no matter how cleanly it had been eviscerated. I still needed to pay the peach farmer something.

I tried again to appraise the value of the peach. It had begun to feel as dead heavy as the chickens displayed on the table before me. I was still frustrated by the farmer's unaccountable meanness, even more irritated by my own misguided belief that I could revive a delicate memory of my young family by tasting a single peach. I thanked the women chicken farmers for their time, turned around, and walked back to the peach table. All around me, people shuffled their feet, lowered their eyes as they offered their five-dollar bills, and received full bags of Big Reds. I fumbled in my purse, pulled out a wad of dollars. I handed the uncounted bills over to the farmer, and said, "I don't know what it's worth, but I can't take your peach for free."

He nodded, his face no less stony. I turned, walked back through the market and out to the railroad station, where new mothers sat behind an iron railing, holding infants and toddlers on their laps, waiting for a train to pass. I stopped walking, unable to join them. I felt vaguely that I'd moved past this stage of my own life, that I might feel like an intruder standing among those who were still in it. I stood at a distance, down in the rail bed among the stones and rusty railroad spikes. The sky was completely colorless. A vee of black geese rowed through it, heading deeper south, their harsh calls already distant. I began eating the late-season peach. The Big Red was large as a softball, fragrant and soft, but not too soft. Its juices ran properly down to my elbows. But there was a deep nick at the top near the stem, and there was a chemical taste within its flesh. As the Norfolk and Southern charged through, grit blew off its empty freight cars, and the children screamed with terror and delight. Though it passed too quickly, I had just enough time to glimpse the black logo of a young horse rearing up, dancing on the nose of the locomotive.

Loitering in a Field of
Confederate Dead

ON A LATE SUMMER SUNDAY, when it was still searing hot in South Carolina, I took Hunter up into the North Carolina mountains, to Flat Rock to see the 25th North Carolina Infantry perform their ninth annual Civil War re-enactment. As usual we were looking for a fun yet instructive way to escape the flatland heat, some small amusement that would occupy us for an entire languid afternoon.

Before going, I battled with myself before taking my son to this event. I worried about the long-term effect a war scene might have on him. A tender-hearted four year old, he broke out the first aid kit whenever our Main Coon struggled with a hairball. Still, though we never allowed him toy weapons, I'd catch him stealing ripe bananas from the fruit bowl, aiming them like pistols at the same cat. I called a friend from Alabama, who said, "You can't damage that boy's psyche by taking him to a Civil War re-enactment." I gave in. Though we'd lived in South Carolina for five years, the local customs still seemed foreign and exotic. Secretly, I harbored an armchair interest in this popular ritual.

I parked a few miles from the Carl Sandburg home, paid my five dollars, and we were in. Hunter pulled me through the encampment. We bypassed the preacher who read from the Book of Job and played "Going for a Soldier" on the harmonica. We stepped into the ladies' fashion show tent, entering a swirl of silk taffeta ball gowns with puffed sleeves and impossibly tiny waists. We strolled at a distance from a lady trussed up in a dark petticoat with a hoop skirt, gloves and bonnet. Fluttering a sandalwood fan, she gave a demonstration of the lined bodice and sleeves of a typical day dress, the layers of fabric that pulled perspiration away from the body in summers, and a liner that served well as winter insulation. I lingered near a black satin mourning gown, completed by a black lace cap. I stopped completely in the underpinnings section, marveled at a full, 12-bone corset, and re-read the sign beside it that announced, "Ladies, if you've spent your life searching for the perfect corset, Look No Further!"

As I was contemplating the kind of twentieth-century woman who'd search her entire life for a perfect corset, Hunter tugged at my arm, and we were out of the tent. I didn't try to slow him down. At this age, Hunter always ran through the halls of art and history museums, yelling, "I beat you! I beat you!" as if there were a finish line somewhere at the other end. How could I have expected a tour of living history to be any different?

We stopped at the battlefield as the 25th Cavalry rode down the hill from their encampment. We squatted on a hillside overlooking the battle scene. Soon we were joined by two children—an eight-year-old girl dressed in a petticoat and violet hair ribbons, a younger boy with a popgun. They offered to share their hot-dogs and grilled turkey legs with us.

"Who's going to win today?" the girl said.

"My daddy says the rebels," the boy said. "The Yankees won yesterday."

"They didn't take turns winning like that in the real war, you know," the girl said.

From these children, I learned that no one wants to be a Union soldier in North Carolina. To be fair, the troops must trade off days wearing the navy flannel. Secondly, both sides number off before each battle—if a soldier calls an even number he'll live; if he calls odd, he'll join the ranks of the Confederate dead. These children knew the drills and maneuvers their fathers performed on the battlefield. They cheered them on the way most fans applaud at football games.

"Kill those Yankees," the girl yelled.

"Shoot them. Shoot them," Hunter joined in.

Below us, a pine board cabin had been built in the center of the battlefield. A few feet away, dried corn husks tied to ten metal poles were speared into two rows in the ground. A group of women in petticoats filed into the cabin, guarded by a couple of Confederate foot soldiers.

One woman yelled, "If you come any closer, I'll shoot you." Then the group broke up laughing.

"Hey, do you want to go into the cabin after it's done burning?" the little girl said.

"Okay," the boy said.

As the cavalry road by, Hunter and I scooted back a few feet. Though I grew up just above Kentucky horse country, I've always been in awe of horses, fearful of their tall powerful haunches and stomping hooves. Sensing this, Hunter climbed into my lap.

"I'm scared," he said.

"Do you want to go home?" I said.

"No, I'm not scared anymore," he said.

The Union cavalry shot the two rebel foot soldiers in the head and marched the women off the field, toward the medical tent. They tossed a lit torch into the cabin. Black smoke and flames billowed out of the roof, and the thin wood burned and snapped.

As I watched the scene, I realized that war must have been terribly boring. On the field, the front lines stood facing each other, waiting to shoot, and to be shot at. Though there was plenty of gunfire, very few men fell. They lingered about, as though waiting for something to happen—as though they'd forgotten that we were all watching from the hillside. Loitering is the only word I can use to describe the scene before me. Over a loud speaker, the company historian recited obscure trivia and well-known Civil War facts. Ulysses S. Grant was a real drinker who filled his troops' canteens with whiskey; there was no such thing as a little drummer boy. No one below the age of seventeen ever fought.

A wave of heat singed my eyes and cheeks. Hunter and I backed farther away from the field. The walls of the cabin collapsed beneath flames, and the fire spread quickly, blackening the dry brittle grass. A man in a chef's hat ran onto the field; he'd been cooking hot-dogs behind the refreshment tent. He carried a dishpan of water and doused the flaming patches of grass. I measured the distance between the spreading fire and the bodies of the dead soldiers still lying twenty feet from the cabin. I remembered that at nighttime, in the Battle of the Wilderness, the troops had lain awake listening to their wounded scream as they burned to death in brush fire. Disappointed by the collapsed cabin, my son's new friend stood, hiked up her skirt, and pushed a sweaty strand of hair from her eyes. She patted Hunter on the head. "I'm going to the medical tent now."

"Get up," I yelled down to the soldiers. "The fire's spreading."

The chef knelt beside the soldiers who'd been shot in the head, whispering in their ears. The dead men stood, and staggered away from the fire, into the shade of a willow tree near the enemy line.

"Those men are idiots, aren't they?" Hunter said. He also called people who rode motorcycles without helmets idiots. To him, anyone who risked his own personal safety were grouped under this name.

"No, honey," I said. "This is different. Those men were just play-ing. Nobody got hurt."

But how could I explain what we'd just seen? We'd gone willingly into the heavenly North Carolina mountains. We'd seen dead soldiers rise and limp into the safe shade of willows. We'd shared hot-dogs with kind children whose fathers loitered in a field of Confederate dead. We'd had a good day. On the way home, my son slept in his car seat, his face flushed with sun and tired happiness. I glanced back at him every few miles, and wondered how I would ever keep him safe.

Appalachian Wedding Cake

I CAME TO KNOW MY MOTHER-IN-LAW, Mary, through the recipes she gave to me. In my memory, I always see and hear Mary in the kitchen of the two-story brick house my father-in-law built after he retired from the Norfolk and Southern Railroad, in the mountain town of Bluefield, Virginia, where Mary had lived all her life, and raised her five children. When Rick and I went back to Virginia for a visit, Mary and I often woke before dawn and sat across from each other at the kitchen table, waiting for the sun to rise, and for the rest of the house to wake. Sometimes, we peeled apples together. Rick's grandmother still lived back on the family's home place, on a ridge between a limestone quarry and the town's cemetery. Below the grandmother's house was a green apple tree that continually dropped spotted, lopsided apples onto the gravel drive leading to the grandmother's house. Rick's father wouldn't throw any of the fallen fruit away. Summers, he brought home a bushel of bruised apples every evening, after he'd been up to check on his mother.

Mary and I would stand in the morning quiet of her kitchen, peeling and discarding the damaged spots off each apple. We dropped the good slices into a pot of water, sugar, cinnamon and cloves, boiling this mixture into dark brown apple butter. While the apples simmered, Mary baked six thin layers of a gingery molasses cake, three at a time, in three well-seasoned cast iron skillets. When the cake layers cooled, she stacked them, frosting each layer with the apple butter. The cake was supposed to "age" for a day, so that the apple butter could soak into the spiced layers until they became sweet and delicate. Nobody in the house ever waited for this cake to age. They ate it young, right after supper, which was always served at midday at my in-laws' house.

Mary called this dessert molasses cake, or apple stack cake. Though she made this cake for all kinds of family gatherings, it was once the traditional wedding cake at Appalachian weddings. The brides who lived on the remote sides of these Southern mountains relied on their guests to bring a thin layer of molasses cake when they arrived at the wedding. The brides' mothers would assemble the cake, and spread apple butter between the layers. It is said that the popularity of the bride determined the final height of the cake.

This is a humble-looking cake that most women of this region make without a written recipe. It's not difficult. It requires only the patience for simmering a bushel of apples into butter, and waiting for six layers of cake to bake. While we waited for the cake layers to cool, Mary often told stories about her family. She'd grown up in a trailer on the other side of Bluefield, on a ridge known locally as Dump Hill. My father-in-law always said that Mary's early upbringing was so rough that the details of what happened to her as a child on Dump Hill could not be repeated. Though she hardly ever spoke of herself, Mary told stories about the women of her family. These women married young and faced almost unendurable hardships—poverty, abandonment, violence—and endured.

Perhaps the bitterness of Mary's past was what prompted her to adore anything sweet. Perhaps her own hardscrabble childhood and early marriage made her into the genuinely kind mother woman who readily adopted me as her daughter-in-law, and taught me how to make the Appalachian wedding cake recipe she'd learned from her own mother-in-law.

When Mary passed away from cancer, Rick's father began making all of Mary's dessert recipes—brown sugar fudge, chess pie, and banana pudding—for the family. The last time Rick and I visited Virginia, I woke early and found Rick's father in the kitchen. The whole house smelled warmly of the ginger and molasses cakes that he'd been baking while the rest of the house slept. As he assembled and iced the cake layers, his grizzled face softened, turning almost boyish. I could tell he was remembering Mary, perhaps recalling her as a young wife, still healthy enough to stand in that kitchen for hours, peeling those homely apples, baking those humble layers of cake. Larry had baked his cake layers in different sized skillets, and he'd iced the layers with cooked apples rather than apple butter. The finished cake looked a bit like a lopsided beehive, but there was no mistaking. It was an Appalachian wedding cake. We ate it "young," drizzled with caramel, and dusted with powdered sugar.

Just For Fun

"Their sons grow suicidally beautiful"
　　--James Wright, "Autumn Begins in Martins Ferry, Ohio"

IN LATE AUGUST, THE SATURDAY BEFORE LABOR DAY, I walked down my
driveway in the middle of the afternoon to pull my garbage can back to
the house. I walked slowly, breathing the thick, wet air that came out of
the woods that flanked the backs of the houses across the street. It had
been a summer of Biblical rains in South Carolina. The weathermen had
counted nearly forty days and forty nights of unrelenting downpours.
Now the rain had stopped, and the heat had taken over. All around
me, tulip poplars and oaks had dropped limbs during the storms, and
the limbs had been soaked so deeply that the heartwood within them
had decayed, and white lichen grew out of the soft wood. I stood at the
edge of my driveway, examined a large spider that had come out of the
woods and spun its web over the handle of my garbage can, and tried to
determine whether it had the violin markings of a brown recluse, or the
red hourglass of a black widow. Just as I decided it was safe to touch
the handle, where the spider sat harmlessly in the middle of its web,
two boys walked out of the woods, carrying black assault-style weapons.

I'd never seen these boys before. They looked about fourteen or
fifteen. They both were dressed in military camouflage. They walked
languidly, blending with the hazy greens and browns of the woods across
the street. I live about a mile from the local hunt club, in gun country,
and though I don't own a gun, I know plenty of people who do. I know
enough to identify high-powered ones when I see them. The tall, slender
boy carried what appeared to be a semi-automatic rifle, resting against
his shoulder. The shorter one swung what looked like a large-caliber
handgun near his hip. When they saw me, they stopped and shuffled
their feet, as if silently deciding something between themselves. The
shorter one lifted his black pistol, pointed it at me. He turned it in slow

circles, his finger on the trigger. My mind hazy with fear, I watched the boy brandish the gun, his impassive face blending with his camouflage suit. He watched steadily for my reaction. In that moment I felt—just as deeply as the fear and panic welling through my body—the boys' desire to see my terror. It would be good fun for both boys to see me cry, run or scream for help, a diversion from summer boredom, this inexorable heat between rainstorms.

I stood unarmed, in a T-shirt, gym shorts, and a pair of running shoes, but I didn't run away. I felt an unreasonable stubbornness, some animal instinct that steadied me. I didn't want to be a source of amusement to them. I lowered my eyes, grabbed the garbage can handle, and began pulling it slowly across the grass. I walked backwards. At the very least, I thought, I wouldn't be shot in the back. I stole glances at them as I moved toward my house. The shorter boy lowered his pistol. He looked a bit disappointed. The taller one raised his semi-automatic rifle and shot off a round, straight into the sky. The shots rang like buckshot rattling up the long barrel, muted as if by a pillow of air. Both boys laughed and walked on down the road. The shorter one waved his pistol one last time in my direction. He called out to me in a way that sounded almost friendly, "Later, Y'all," as if we'd just shared a fun moment together.

They disappeared around the bend in the road where the woods meet the street corner beneath a basketball goal where most of the neighborhood kids play. I went inside my house. In the kitchen, I realized I'd been sweating so hard that I'd soaked my shirt. A quaking had begun deep inside of me, and I could feel my whole body begin to shake, but I tamped down the shaking. Even out of their sight, I didn't want to give way to the terror those boys had wanted to see in me. I certainly didn't want to alarm Rick. But I needed to tell someone, preferably an adult who might be able to make sense out of what had just happened.

Rick was raised with guns in the mountains of southwest Virginia. His father had given him a hunting rifle when he was a boy, instructing him to keep it empty and always locked in a gun rack when he wasn't hunting for animals that the family often relied on for food. Rick said that his father took him hunting once, and that he'd seen a doe cry when his father shot her in the chest, and that having to watch that deer die so slowly had killed every bit of his adolescent fascination with firearms. Still, he knew more about guns than I did. I wanted him to advise me about what I should do about the pistol the boy had pointed at me.

I found Rick upstairs, emerging from the shower. Through the half-closed door and shower steam, I mustered the calmest voice I could as I recounted the boys and their guns, how they'd brandished them at me while I was trying to take in the garbage can.

"What?"

As I repeated the story, Rick picked up his phone and car keys.

"Where are you going?" I said.

"I know what I'm doing."

"You're not going after them, are you? They have guns. You don't."

"I know what I'm doing." He walked outside and crossed the lawn.

Later, I learned that Rick first consulted with our next-door neighbor, J.C. A widower who earned his living making dentures, J.C. hadn't been able to spend much time inside his house since his wife died five years before. He'd moved a couch, a refrigerator and a wide-screen t.v. into his garage so that he could live out there, with the garage door open. Nights, when he couldn't sleep, he patrolled the neighborhood in his red Ford pickup. He saw everything, and he knew who everyone in the neighborhood was. He told Rick he recognized the description of the boys, and he knew where they lived.

He also brought a new insight to the situation.

"If those boys had pointed a gun at me or anyone in my family, I'd have shot them. If I were you, I'd call the police." Rick said J.C.'s words made him understand that those guns were lethal-- beyond the fact that they'd brandished them at me. The Stand Your Ground Laws in South Carolina make it legal for people to use deadly force against those they believe to be an assailant. According to this law, people can use any gun within their reach, even one that's not licensed them, to shoot and kill a would-be assailant who crosses onto their property. If those boys had pointed their guns at anyone else in the neighborhood who owned a gun, they risked being shot, maybe killed. Before calling the police,

Rick drove every street of our neighborhood, until he found the boys still carrying the rifle and pistol. He rolled down a window, called out to them, asked if they'd pointed their guns at his wife. They looked him straight in the eye, and denied everything.

If it had been up to me, I wouldn't have called the local police, at least not before I had time to think through what had just happened. The first officer to reach us was a middle-aged man with a bit of Wisconsin in his voice. He informed us that his partner had found the boys, and had already spoken with one of their parents, a father who openly admitted that his children were walking through the neighborhood carrying airsoft guns. I didn't know what an airsoft gun was, so the officer explained that these are replica guns designed for people who want to play with guns that look and sound exactly like highly-lethal weapons, usually AK-47s or large-caliber handguns. The only mark distinguishing airsoft replica guns from "real" assault weapons is an orange slash on the barrel, or an orange tip at the end of the muzzle.

The policeman asked me if I'd seen an orange blaze, or tip, on the barrel of either weapon carried by the boys.

I shook my head. "No, all I saw was black."

He asked me the skin color of the boys, if they were white or black, and I replied, "Honestly, I couldn't tell you their skin color. They were both wearing camouflage. One was tall and thin, the other was shorter. Once I saw those guns, particularly the one that was pointed at me, that's all I saw of them."

I asked the policeman to sit at our dining room table so that he could write on the clipboard he held, and he replied, "I'm not going to be the one writing here." He gave me a sheet of paper and told me to write down what happened, using as many details as possible. For the last twenty years, I've made my living teaching college writing classes, and I always tell my students that it's best not to write in a moment of fear, anger, or any uncontrollable emotion. I tell them that upsetting events are better recounted in moments of relative calm. As I started writing, my heart felt like a glass vase shattered into a thousand fine shreds that shot through every artery, prickling the veins just beneath the surface of my skin. Even still, I knew that once written, my words would be handed over to a lawman, possibly a lawyer. They could be turned on those boys. My hand shook, and I worried about becoming unhinged. I'd lived for so long in gun country, among so many gun people, that I vaguely wondered if I was being unreasonable. Should I have been able to distinguish between a real gun and a fake as the boys were brandishing them at me? Keep calm, I thought. Write only what happened. Leave out any emotions.

As I wrote, Rick and the cop talked about the weather, the torrential rains that had fallen nearly every day that summer, the loss of all the heat-resistant plants in our garden, including our twenty-year-old rosemary that had turned brown and shriveled into the mineral-poor dirt. As the officer and Rick discussed the strange weather, I thought about young men in recent news, bored and armed with assault weapons, who'd gone out to taunt, rob, or kill unarmed victims "just for fun." During the first week of August, on a nearby bike trail, a dozen young men assaulted a young male bicyclist. They pointed a gun at him, kicking and beating him. They aimed a gun at the boy's head, and misfired it. As they walked away with the victim's bike, they dry fired the empty gun into the sky.

I kept writing, telling myself that I was safe. I had not been shot, beaten, or robbed. I kept telling myself to stay calm, to write only what had happened, to leave out any emotions. When I finished, I passed my statement to the policeman. He held the paper with both hands as he read it to himself.

When he finished reading, he looked up. "Why didn't you write down in your statement how the gun sounded when he fired it off?" he said.

"What the gun sounded like isn't the point, is it?" I said. "The point is that those young men pointed lethal-looking guns at me in my own front yard. I'll tell you that both guns looked real, especially the pistol that was pointed at me."

The policeman put the statement down on the table. "You're right," he said. "They bullied and violated you. You felt afraid, and now you're angry. Soon, you may start blaming yourself."

"Of course I was afraid," I said. "But they wanted to see that fear, and I wasn't going to give that to them. And why would I blame myself? I was standing in my own front yard, clearly unarmed, taking in the garbage can."

"Yes, but you might start blaming yourself. You might start thinking that you went outside at the wrong time of the day, or that you somehow put yourself in that position."

"No, I don't think I will," I said.

The officer was just doing his work, and maybe trying to be sympathetic. I realized this even as I spoke to him. I knew for certain that he had, in fact, taken the acts of those two boys seriously when he explained that the young men in question had committed a crime. It's illegal in most states to point a firearm of any kind at a person or her property with the intention of putting a reasonable person in fear of her safety. The policeman said that he would talk to the boys' parents. If he got cooperation from the parents, he would try to get them treated as juvenile offenders. If he didn't get cooperation, he might need to have them tried as adults for assault. I might need to identify them in a police line up, possibly appear in court. As he left, he said it could take a while for any of this to happen, given that it was a holiday weekend. The officer's partner, a younger man with a crew cut, had just arrived as the first officer was leaving. He chimed in, "Yeah, and there's also the fact that the force will be dealing with a real shooting that happened across town this weekend."

My face filled with heat. Waves of anger welled through me as the second officer's words clarified why I'd felt reluctant to call the local police. I imagined trying to identify the two boys at the police station, and felt sure that I'd be unable to identify them because I'd been staring only at their guns. I imagined sitting through a court session, if it came to that. I was pretty certain I'd be treated like an hysteric who was too ignorant to recognize the difference between a real gun and a "toy." Never mind that the guns had looked so real that nobody but a trained police officer—an armed man who had the benefit of examining them up close for an extended period of time—could tell that they were unreal. The officer's younger partner may as well have called my case, "The non-real shooting." The older officer, however sympathetic, had told me not to blame myself. When a person tells you not to blame yourself, it usually means someone, at some point, will assign you blame.

I didn't blame myself for what had happened, but the time for blaming did come a couple of hours later, as I talked with Rick. He'd turned on the t.v. in the den. He was watching the ongoing news coverage of the bombings in Syria, the nearly impossible decisions President Obama would need to make when dealing with a government that fired chemical weapons on its own people. When he saw me, he turned the station to the Virginia Tech football game, and lowered the volume.

"I don't want to send two boys to prison," he said.

"I don't either."

"I wasn't going to call the police, but when I saw the guns, they looked so real...." He trailed off. "If they'd admitted what they'd done, I would've just gone to speak to their parents, but they denied everything."

"It was the way they handled the guns, as if they were playing a game with me, as if I weren't completely real to them," I said. "That was worse than the guns themselves."

"I keep thinking of the guns we had in our house when I was a kid. My father would never have let me carry a loaded gun around our neighborhood. I never would have walked down the street and pointed my hunting rifle at a neighbor."

"No, but you're from a different era. You were raised by different parents."

"I blame their parents," Rick said. "What kind of parents would buy their teenaged children guns that are exact replicas of assault-style weapons? Maybe those boys did what any normal teenager raised in the South would do if he were given a firearm like that. Maybe they just weren't thinking."

"We have a teenage son," I said. "He was born and raised here. He never asked for an assault-style replica firearm. We never bought him one. He'd never walk down the street and point a gun at a neighbor."

"No, he wouldn't," Rick said.

We agreed not to tell Hunter about the gun incident. He was away

63

at college in Nashville, and news of this sort would only make him worry about me. It might even make him nervous about walking around his own college campus. Already, he was more cautious than Rick or I had ever been when we were in college, perhaps because he'd grown up in a gun culture. He was in middle school when the Virginia Tech massacre occurred, and since then he'd followed news of the Fort Hood massacre, the Aurora Theater shooting and, most recently, Sandy Hook.

"Parents are supposed to protect children." Rick paused, started again. "But if I'd seen those boys pointing guns at you or Hunter, if I still had a gun, I might have shot them." He looked down at his hands, his face filled with anger and confusion.

I went upstairs. Passing my son's room, I looked through the doorway, taking in his narrow bed, neat and undisturbed, his first guitar resting in its stand, the scent of boy still lingering in the air. I sifted through his bookshelves, paging through the books he'd treasured growing up—Steinbeck's *The Pearl*, Orwell's *1984*, and every book by Tolkien. My son had needed to leave behind a number of books in order to save dorm room space for his guitars, but he'd taken a volume of Orwell essays with him. Though he spent the better part of his days happily filling his mind with a steady stream of bass chords and arpeggios, he'd recently confessed that there were times when there were so many complicated patterns of music in his head at once that he felt overwhelmed, and in need of diversion. Once, when this happened, he'd taken out his favorite Orwell essay, "Shooting An Elephant," and had one of his roommates read it to him. I was pleased when he told me this, relieved that he'd chosen to amuse and becalm himself with an essay about the conflict between the law and an individual's moral conscience under an imperialist government.

As I examined my own conscience, I knew exactly how I would have felt if I'd seen those boys pointing an assault-style weapon of any kind at my son. I would have wanted them punished and put away forever. But the gun was pointed at me, and this fact complicated my feelings. I'm an adult, a mother and an educator who believes that parents should protect children—even the ones who aren't their own. What these kids had done to me was frightening, but if I took myself out of the picture,

I could see how their actions were disturbing and potentially self-destructive. Somehow, the adults in their lives had failed to apprise them of one of the very basic laws that govern civilized behavior: you do not point any kind of firearm at other people with the intention of frightening them. Pointing firearms at people should never be a source of your own amusement.

I went into my office and closed the door. As I turned on my computer I felt as if I were about to commit my own transgression. By this time, the boys, their guns, and even the police statement had begun to feel like an illicit secret Rick and I would not speak about again. It was as if, silently, we'd agreed to expel all boys with guns from our conversation. We would not allow them to remain in our home by speaking of them. We would not allow them to wield that power over us.

This didn't stop me from thinking about them while alone, wondering if a real crime had been committed that day, and if it warranted punishment or prison. We've all seen stories of young men wielding real assault weapons, on shooting sprees, yet I'd never heard about kids on the loose with these airsoft assault rifle replicas.

According to the International Association of Chiefs of Police, the airsoft look-alikes are considered a threat to public safety in most developed countries outside the United States. The guns are considered lethal because, as criminal misuse of assault weapons increases, police are more likely to assume that look-alike airguns are real firearms. People who thoughtlessly brandish look-alike firearms run the risk of finding themselves in a face-off with a police officer who must make a split decision on whether to draw a weapon, and fire. Replica airsoft guns have become so realistic in the last few years that they've been used by the military in training maneuvers because the replicas have the same heft and design as the assault weapons they will use in combat. Police officers began practicing deadly force maneuvers with them. Then police forces stopped using the airguns because too many recruits, unable to distinguish between the real guns and airguns, took their real guns into training sessions by mistake, and maimed each other while practicing deadly force.

Airsoft guns are considered illegal in countries such as Korea,

Malaysia, Thailand, and Singapore. Canada prohibits the importation of "replica" airsoft guns. In the United States airsoft guns are considered toys. Though it's illegal for a child under 18 to purchase them, it's legal for children of all ages to play with them. There's only one Federal regulation placed upon airsoft guns in America. Federal importation laws in the United States mandate the presence of a minimum 6 mm wide blaze orange tip on any airsoft gun imported into the country or transported within the states. However, state laws vary on whether you can remove the orange tip on an airgun. It's common practice for airgun enthusiasts to remove the blazes in order to simulate more completely the "real" experience of shooting at targets, including other human beings.

The most common rhetoric used by those who are against placing regulations upon replica assault weapons in the U.S. is that these would be "feel good laws" put into place by "anti-gun hysterics" who "lack common sense." Scrolling through news articles, I discovered a study on airguns done by the Centers for Disease Control and Prevention in 2005. According to this study, approximately 19,675 non-powder gun injuries were treated in U.S. emergency rooms. Of these injuries, 71 percent involved individuals aged 20 or under. I also found an abundance of stories about children across the United States who were arrested, irreversibly maimed, or killed because they'd used an alarming lack of common sense while mishandling airsoft guns.

On December 19, 2010, *The Los Angeles Times* reported that an LAPD officer shot a 13-year-old boy playing with an air soft gun after dark. The officer commanded that the boy show his hands, but the boy kept concealing his weapon in his sweatshirt pocket. When he finally revealed the gun, the officer could not see the orange blaze on the tip, and he shot the boy in self-defense. The bullet struck the boy's spine and shattered the vertebrae in his upper chest, pulverizing this spinal cord and leaving him paralyzed from the upper chest down.

On January 8, 2012, *The New York Times* reported a story of a 15-year-old eighth grader who'd assaulted another student while carrying a high-powered replica black Glock semi-automatic. When teachers asked if he was carrying a gun, he said he was. When the police arrived and told the boy to put down his gun, he didn't comply. They shot him in the chest and abdomen. He was pronounced dead by the time he reached the hospital.

On April 23, 2013, the *New York Post* reported that a 20-year-old NYU psychology student named Bernard Goal was arrested and charged for illegal weapon possession after police discovered that he had turned his Manhattan dorm room into "an air rifle factory." The public safety officers found four airsoft weapons that closely resembled AK-47s and a black Colt carbine rifle in his dorm room. Goal was assembling the weapons with parts he bought online, selling the guns for $500 each to other students on campus. NYPD officers charged him with six violations of a local law that prohibits the possession or sale of air rifles and replica firearms.

After about an hour of reading stories like these, I determined that although children in the U.S. under the age of 18 cannot legally buy airsoft guns, they've been committing adult crimes of rage, greed, and madness with them for years. Mentally unbalanced teens have been committing suicide by police, intentionally bringing replica airguns to school, and drawing them on classmates. When armed officers arrive at the scene, the police unwittingly shoot, and often kill them in front of all the other students. More disturbingly, American air rifle companies target their ads toward children and adolescents, profiting off those who aren't old enough to own real assault weapons.

At Airgundepot.com, an online store that specializes in selling air rifles and guns that are indistinguishable from fully operational assault weapons, I found children's starter gun packages for sale. I also found ads for airguns designed to look indistinguishable from UZI Assault pistols, Colt M-16s, and AK-47s. The advertising on this site emphasizes the accuracy of detail, the excitement of owning authentic reproductions of American-made semi-automatic defense weapons. On the main page of this site, the marketing copy reads: "It's 1200 hours and you need to suit up for your next mission. What is going to be your role in your squad as you attack the enemy? Are you going to be the CQB specialist busting down doors and clearing rooms? The Assault Soldier who's (sic) job is to only search and destroy? Will you lay down more rounds of ammo than the enemy combined as support personal (sic)?

Or will you sit in the shadows quietly placing your shots, taking out targets one by one saying, "Boom Headshot" after each kill?" Below this copy, the weapons for sale are divided into "Close Quarters Battle," "Assault," "Support," and "Marksman."

I clicked on the link for assault weapons. Then, I decided to see what would happen if I added an assault weapon to my shopping cart. I clicked on a UTG Multi-Shot Combat Tactical Shotgun, and it was added to my cart. Then, just to see how many guns I could buy, I loaded up my cart with eight different ultra-realistic, high-velocity replica assault weapons, including a Thompson Submachine Gun, an Aftermath Kraken Police Tactical Assault Rifle, and a 60th Anniversary AK-47 that was guaranteed to be indistinguishable from the "infamous" assault rifle Mikhail Timofeevich Kalashnikov designed for The Red Army while he was recovering from his wounds incurred in the Battle of Bryansk.

I proceeded to checkout. My purchase totaled $796.75, and I was guaranteed free ground shipping since I'd ordered more than $179 in firearms. The site asked for my shipping address and informed me I could pay with my Discover, Visa, MasterCard or American Express credit card. The merchant assured me that this was a "secure shopping site," and asked if I'd like to rate my purchase on Yahoo. I did not need to set up an adult account with this company, and I was never asked to verify my age at any point during the ordering process.

I didn't buy $796.75 worth of replica assault weapons that night. I still have no desire to own a gun—real or replica. But I could see how easily an underage paramilitary enthusiast, especially one who is unsupervised by an adult, could acquire a whole arsenal of ultra-realistic replica weapons. All it took was a credit card and access to the Internet. It seems that the American manufacturers of replica airguns are partly to blame for the rise of this peculiar, and often deadly, kind of child's play. Recognizing that plain old hunting rifles or Western six-shooters are no longer as fun to play with, these companies have tapped into the machine gun and large-caliber handgun market, targeting children, or child-minded adults, promising that they too can be just like snipers and soldiers engaged in lethal skirmishes. Their prices are affordable, but they don't account for the cost of children raised on fantasies of battle and big firepower, young men, or women, who could be arrested, maimed, or killed for mishandling their lethal-looking merchandise.

I scrolled through stories until well after sunset, into the raw hours, until my clenched teeth ached, and my eyes were too gritty to stare at a computer screen any longer. The morning's immediate fear had softened into embarrassment, and, oddly, guilt. Now that I'd pressed charges against them, I didn't want to send two boys to prison, or even to see them placed in juvenile detention. I did want to see them properly educated. I felt firmly that I wanted the local police to tell them that it is wrong to point a gun at another human being. I wanted them to be taught that their actions could be dangerous, potentially lethal. I thought, naively, that I would have a say in this matter when the local police called to inform me of any criminal proceedings, juvenile or adult.

Instead, a few days later, a man from the county sheriff's office called and spoke his name so quickly that I didn't have time to write it down, or remember it. He said he was calling to question me about "the incident that happened" in my neighborhood. One of the attending police officers had gone over to the house where the boys lived, and identified their weapons as airsoft guns. The officer on the phone began his line of questioning where my written statement had ended.

"What did the rifle sound like?"

I knew the answer he wanted, that the gunshot sounded unreal. But the guns had looked real, and my fear had been real, and that was the point I knew he was trying to dismiss. My stomach clenched, and I began shaking all over again—this time out of anger, rather than fear. I lowered my voice so that the officer wouldn't hear it trembling. I attempted to make him understand what it felt like to be unarmed and staring down the wrong end of what looked like a real, military-grade gun.

"Two boys came out of the woods, wearing military camouflage, carrying assault-style weapons," I said. "One brandished what looked like a high-caliber pistol at me. Then, the other one shot off the rifle into the air."

"We found the boys," he said. "They were friends of a boy who lives in your neighborhood. They were just playing with those guns. They said they never pointed them at anyone."

"But they lied," I said, regretting the increasingly shrill sound of my voice.

"If we could arrest all people for lying, we wouldn't have any place in our jails to put them."

"Isn't it against the law to point a firearm of any kind at a person?"

"It's only a crime if the gun is real."

"Isn't the definition of criminal assault to cause one person to feel fear or apprehension?"

"Well, then you'd have to prove that they wanted to make you feel afraid."

"Pointing an assault-style weapon at me at close range isn't proof that they wanted to make me feel afraid?"

"No, it would only be criminal assault if they shot at you."

"So, you're saying that I needed to be shot at before I could prove that they intended to frighten me?"

"Yes, ma'am," he said. "There is a case in another neighborhood that we are looking into. Some kids fired on some other unarmed kids with airsoft guns, but we got the kids to apologize to the kids they shot at and their families. Now everything is all right."

That was not play, I thought. Children firing loaded guns at other kids was never going to be all right. "Isn't it a Federal crime to remove the orange blazes from an airsoft gun?" I asked.

"We don't have any regulations against that here," he said. "The Feds might could deal with that."

What disturbed me about this conversation was this officer's determination to prove that since the gun aimed at me was not defined as a real firearm in the U.S., the boys had no real intentions of frightening me, and therefore, my fear was unreal. I heard the blame in what he was not saying. I was fairly certain he'd already identified me as one of those "anti-gun hysterics" who lacked common sense. I decided to circle back to the convictions I'd come to the night of "the incident that happened in my neighborhood." I wanted to at least make him see how lethal the boys' behavior might have been to themselves.

"You know, the main reason my husband called the police was because most of our neighbors own real firearms," I said. "The guy next door said he would have shot those boys if they'd pulled their guns on him or any member of his family.   He would have been within his legal rights to do this."

"Yeah, there are all kinds of kids getting bloodied up right now because they're pointing airsoft guns at police officers, and the police are firing on them."

"So you're not going to talk to the boys and make them understand that it's wrong and dangerous to point a replica firearm at someone? I don't want to see two kids go to prison, but I'd like to see them educated."

"I wish we could."

"So the case is closed?"

"Yes, it's closed."

"And you're not going to do anything about it?"

"You just said yourself that you didn't want anything done about it."

"I said I didn't want to send two boys to prison. I said I'd like to see them educated about how their actions showed poor judgment, and could have been lethal."

"You could hire a lawyer, but you'd have to prove that they tried to make you afraid. In your case, it would be hard to prove that."

"What if they come back?" I said. "What if their parents get angry that I called the police, and they come back with real guns?"

"Well, if they come back with their guns, you just call us up, and we'll start this all over again."

I thanked the officer for his time and hung up, feeling frustrated, and vaguely bullied. I felt certain that I'd never call the local police again, for any reason. I was startled by the officer's lack of diplomacy, disturbed by how much my moral conscience differed from this local lawman's. I was profoundly disappointed by my own inability to convince him that I was a person with an ordinary degree of reason. I'd failed to prove that I possessed the ability to look at the situation with any amount of objectivity. I went downstairs and told my husband that the case was closed, that the boys had lied, and that the law enforcement officers had not taken their actions seriously because the assault firearms were not "real."

Rick said that we could only hope that the boys with the replica airguns were good kids, and that a visit from the police would scare them enough so that they'd realize the danger of their actions. I didn't know these kids, or whether they were "good" or "bad," though their actions indicated bad judgment that might some day lead to worse consequences. Would they go out again and point their replica air weapons at someone who carried a real gun, possibly a police officer, and would that gunman shoot them? Would their adolescent romance with assault-style replica firearms evolve into adult fanaticism with assault weapons?

Though I promised myself that I wouldn't live in unreasonable fear of guns, I continued to feel the specter of weapons. The gun pointed at me was "unreal," but the issue of gun regulations, or the lack of them, in the U.S. had become real and personal. I began to see the thread that connects large and small incidents that involve the misuse of guns. In the weeks following the replica gun incident in my own neighborhood, I watched the news of the mass shooting at the Washington Navy Shipyard. Flags were flown at half-staff for the twelve victims. The pundits' familiar blaming began: the young gunman suffered from mental illness and watched too many video games. Appeals for increased gun regulations in the U.S. were made then quickly muted by the din of pro-gun advocates who blamed the naval facility for having inadequate security procedures, suggesting that the "gun-free zone" on this military base was to blame for this massacre. They cried out for more guns, claiming that the tragedy would have been averted if the "good guys" with guns had been able to shoot at the shooter.

Though I was in no immediate danger of this "real" grand-scale shooting, I felt a general uneasiness with the media's "good guy-bad-guy" rhetoric, and the mentality of those who fight the smallest efforts towards gun control in the United States. How can we know the minds and souls of every human being who owns a gun in America? How can a shoot out between the "good" and "bad" owners of guns be a reasonable and safe response to a mass shooting? Why not simply increase gun regulation so that real and replica semi-automatic weapons don't land in the hands of those who handle them recklessly? While watching news stories about mass shootings in shopping malls, schools, and movie theaters, or children killed by police who mistook their replica automatic weapons for real ones, my eyes would become gritty and begin to water. I'd feel overly warm, almost queasy, disturbed but not shocked. I'd shut the news off, and feel the need for open air.

I began taking reasonable precautions that anyone living in the twenty-first century, in the middle of gun country, must take when walking outside her own house. I stopped taking walks in my neighborhood. I'd wait to check our mailbox when other adults were home from work, or when a few mothers were outside, watching their kids play along the street. Weeks, then months, passed. My mind eased about the possibility that those two boys might return to my house. I almost forgot about them.

In late August of the following year, they came back. That afternoon, I'd been watching a story on t.v. about a nine-year-old girl who accidentally shot and killed her gun instructor with an Uzi at a shooting range called "Bullets and Burgers" in Dolan Springs, Arizona, a gun fun park an hour outside of Las Vegas that prides itself for having a "unique Desert Storm atmosphere and military-style bunkers." The girl's parents paid for her to have a good time with an Israeli-made submachine gun. But her body was too small to handle the gun's recoil, the Uzi got away from her, and she shot the shooting instructor in the head.

The mother of the girl who shot and killed thirty-nine-year old Charles Vacca, the gun instructor, had been filming her daughter with her cell phone while she practiced shooting the Uzi. When it became clear that her daughter had shot a man in the head, the mother took her to a nearby hotel so that she would not see the results of what she'd done, and become traumatized. I couldn't help but wonder why the girl's parents thought it would be fun to put an Uzi in the hands of their small daughter, and then film her. Hadn't they considered the possible repercussions of their own actions before the shooting occurred? Though the child remained in no danger of going to prison for murder, I wondered about the ways she'd be marked forever by this ghastly event.

The familiar queasiness set in. The room felt too warm, and the doors and windows of my house seemed smaller. I walked outside and down my driveway to check the mail. All around me droughted-out trees dropped golden leaves. My neighbors had raked them into dusty piles along the sides of the road. I looked up, and saw the boys standing beside my mailbox. They weren't wearing camouflage this time, and they weren't carrying guns. They'd grown up a bit since I'd last seen them. They were young men now. They weren't laughing. They stood in the street and stared at me, their eyes unapologetic, their hands empty of any gesture that might convince me they'd returned with friendly intentions.

At first I felt an eerie recognition, the surreal symmetry of seeing them standing in the same spot I'd seen them in almost exactly a year before. I realized I would have recognized them if they'd appeared before me in a police line up. I realized, too, that the officer from the county sheriff's department I'd talked with over the phone had been wrong about their intentions the summer before. The boys had wielded their guns with the intention of terrifying me. I knew this because when they'd been carrying firearms, I had feared them. Now that they were unarmed, I was no longer afraid.

Though they weren't pointing guns at me this time, I felt marked by these two young men. Their names had been kept from me because they were minors, but I suspected they knew exactly who I was--the hysterical lady who called the police on them the summer before, the unreasonable one who didn't know enough to distinguish their toys from real guns. They could return to find me any time they wanted, more times than I cared to think about. They must have been told not to carry their replica firearms around in public, but I wondered what they'd been taught, if anything.

I wish now that I'd had a generous enough character to forgive them. I wish I'd been able to speak to them calmly and reasonably, maybe even offer them a book from my son's shelf, put something in their minds and hands that would relieve them of their blankness and boredom. But in that moment I could only stand there, glaring at them, my mind filled with mute hostility. The taller one bobbed his head, as if he were growing wary of me.

We stood like this for a full minute. Then I heard a muffled shot, and a shattering. I jumped, my head snapping towards two gray ground doves darting out of a pile of fallen leaves at the side of the road. The sound rattled through me like an aftershock, and my arms and legs weakened with phantom panic. I decided the boys needed to go. I placed my hands on my hips, and stared back at them until they began to move along slowly. They stopped every few feet to glance back over their shoulders, shaking their heads. They didn't wave goodbye this time. They didn't holler out, "Later, Y'all."

When they finally disappeared into the woods, I stood at the edge of my driveway, feeling the loss of small civilities. I didn't know why the boys had come back, but I knew that they would always return to me through the sound of a gunshot, real or imagined, and that I would never feel entirely as safe as before my encounter with them. I could feel autumn beginning--the heat breaking, the trees dropping more curdled leaves across the road. Another boy pedaled by on his bike. He looked about fourteen, tall and slender, his skinny arms and legs ungainly. I took a good look at his face. It was open and innocent. He wobbled a little, then righted himself, grabbing the handles on his bike. Once steadied, he lifted a careful hand, waving hello as he passed by. He disappeared beneath the basketball goal at the edge of the woods.

Survivors

ONE EARLY SEPTEMBER, a writer friend who taught English at a small college an hour south from the Carolina town where I live called me up and asked if I would help her rescue some books. My friend had found boxes of Penguin paperbacks stacked from floor to ceiling at her local thrift store. Someone had tried to donate them to the nearby county correctional facility, but the prison had a strict policy against allowing paperbacks in its library. Apparently, this prison would only allow its prisoners to read hardbound editions. When the prison wouldn't take the paperbacks, somebody dumped them off at the thrift store. My friend was browsing this shop when she stumbled upon the storekeeper dragging the boxes of books out the back door. Unable to sell the books, the storekeeper was preparing to burn them in a steel drum in her parking lot.

"How many are there?" I asked over the phone.

"I don't know," my friend said. "A lot. Maybe 5,000? We've got them in a house on campus now. My students took a few, but we've got to move them all by tomorrow."

"What'll happen to the ones you can't give away?" I said.

"We give them back to the store so that they can account for them, something about taxes," she said. "They're going to burn whatever we give back."

She paused, letting me reel from the image of book burning—not for political reasons or censorship, but because nobody wanted them. "There are some good titles left. Why don't you come down and take some?"

The next morning was a Friday. I set out for Clinton, South Carolina, in my black '89 Toyota Corolla, with my son's empty safety seat strapped in the back. All summer, Carolina heat had sucked the air conditioning fluid from my car, and I hadn't yet replaced it. As I drove the country road south, hot September wind swept through the car's open windows. I passed lone horses grazing sun-bleached pastures, ancient oaks bowing beneath a whole summer's weight of kudzu. Unseen cicadas churned inside the trees and roadside ditches, their trills thickening the blue morning air.

Driving through the deep greens and blues of late summer, I felt sweaty and urgent. I dreaded the thought of my friend having to give those books back to a thrift store owner bent on burning them because they would not sell as well as second-hand aluminum Christmas trees, or sets of vintage salt and pepper shakers shaped like friendly Italian chefs. I felt guilty too, greedy for the good titles that might be taken away by the students who'd gone to the campus house filled with books ahead of me. Certain those students were carrying off all the titles that could be mine, I stepped harder on the gas pedal, ignoring the hot gritty air that tore through my hair, the sparse and insignificant speed limit signs, those little white crosses that elegize car crash victims on country roadsides.

I arrived at the college campus and found the white Victorian house where my friend said the books would be. Its lawn and front door were camouflaged by an enormous oriental magnolia whose leaves spooned blooms the size and color of bone china teacups. I tried the door. It was locked, so I walked around back. Pushing open the screen door, I entered the dining room and found the books—classic, modern, and contemporary—stacked on every surface of the room, towering up to the crown molding that flared just beneath the twelve-foot ceiling. I identified titles by Kundera, V.S. Naipaul, and Neruda in the stacks along the dining room table. Over the fireplace mantel, I spied Volumes One and Two of the collected short stories of Somerset Maugham, Dennis Covington's *Salvation on Sand Mountain*, and Carol Shield's *The Stone Diaries*. Copies of Oliver Goldsmith's *The Vicar of Wakefield* and *The Lais of Marie De France* leaned into each other along the window seat below an elegant stained-glass panel.

The room smelled wonderfully of books that spilled into the hallway and up the back stairs to the second floor, but the house was nearly empty of people. Only a couple of students browsed the tables and chairs stacked with books, slipping one or two beneath their arms to take back to their dorm rooms. My friend came into the dining room, and we stood admiring the books, contemplating the bureaucratic whim that nearly destroyed them, the fortunate turn of fate that allowed her to shepherd them into this temporary safe house.

I picked up the Kundera, Naipaul, and Neruda titles and walked over to the fireplace, filling my other arm with my selections from the mantel. I wasn't sure if I would be reading Oliver Goldsmith or the The Lais of Marie De France any time soon, but I collected those too. They were classics, I reasoned. There might come a day when I would regret not having them in my library.

"Are you sure it's okay for me to take all of these?" I said. This was a small, ceremonial question. We both knew that I'd already claimed these books. We both knew that I'd be taking them home.

"Of course," she said.

"Well, I could take a few more back with me, maybe give some away to my students. Do you think that would be okay?"

"Take as many as you want. I've already taken as many as will fit in my apartment. I've got to have them all out of here by this afternoon. We have to give up the space for some Student Life function."

A plan formed. I would take the remaining books in the house, as many as my Corolla would hold, and bring them up to the college where I taught and worked as director of The Writing Center. The following Monday I would announce to the entire campus that there were free books in The Writing Center, that people need only visit to pick them up. This would allow me to place the surviving books in the hands of people more cash poor and book hungry than even I was at this time. It also would remove the stain for those students who were referred to the Writing Center after they'd already failed their writing assignments. These students could come to the center before they failed at writing, without sanction, to find a book they might read for pleasure.

I began stuffing books into my car. I piled them in the front and back as high as I could, without completely obstructing my rear vision, filling the empty child safety seat. Next I put them in the trunk, nestling them around my spare tire. By the time I finished, I'd packed over 2,000 books into my car, so many that my back bumper sagged.

I arrived home in mid-afternoon and unloaded the books into the dining room of my three-bedroom bungalow. I stacked them above and below my dining room table, all along the heart pine window seat. I'd been in such a hurry to rescue the books that I'd stopped sorting through the titles and simply loaded them all into my car; I needed to sort through them all again that weekend, decide which ones I would keep, which ones I would give away. I began putting the books I wanted to keep for myself in the front office of the house, leaving the rest on the dining room floor, beneath the table. All weekend, I shuffled and decided. The pile on my office floor grew as the piles in my dining room shrank.

At some point on Sunday afternoon, I invited over my neighbor, a retired librarian who hailed from a tiny town outside Mobile, Alabama. This town no longer existed, and she spent her days of retirement collecting photographs and documents of people who once lived there, recreating this Dixie ghost town with her memory and research. I told her about the prison library that wouldn't take the paperbacks, the thrift storeowner who'd wanted to burn them. I confessed my inability to part with so many of the rescued books, even though I had no place to put them. My neighbor shook her head, her face impassive. I don't believe she was unmoved, just unsurprised. In her early eighties, she'd already survived three husbands, a child, and her entire hometown. She was used to the relentless tidal rhythm of loss and recovery.

"You're not being greedy for keeping them," she said. "Or, if you are being greedy, you're doing exactly as I would if I were in your place."

She took home a copy of *The Stone Diaries*. I took roughly 1500 books up to the college on Monday morning, leaving the other 500 in my home office. Throughout the day, students and colleagues descended upon the Writing Center, carrying off the books so swiftly that by the time I left at five p.m. there was only a tiny pile left behind. That night, I began double-shelving my own 500 titles on my already-brimming shelves. I took my time, opening one to read its first line, putting it down to read the back cover of another. Soon the piles of books toppled, scattering into heaps. I nested among them, feeling luxurious, and deeply satisfied.

This was my first year working at the college, when I was still new to my duties and prone to taking my professional life home with me. In January of that year, I hosted our first visiting writer-in-residence for the college, Thomas E. Kennedy. A fiction writer from New York City, Tom had lived the last two decades of his life in Copenhagen, writing fiction and working for the Danish Medical Association. It never occurred to me that it was unusual to invite an internationally-acclaimed author into my house for a ham sandwich after I picked him up from the airport. I'd read all of Tom's books before he arrived, and I admired his work tremendously. I knew his writing, and therefore I knew him, or so I believed. It never occurred to me that we would not become friends. After I'd plied Tom with both a ham and a roast beef sandwich, I took him to see my collection of 500 Penguin paperbacks, recounting the saga of how my friend and I rescued them from despotic prison bureaucrats and a fire.

Tom did become a good friend, and he has remained so for nearly two decades. About a month ago, he sent a note, recalling my stash of rescued books that I showed off to him on the day we first met. He wanted my permission to tell the story of "the book rescue" in an essay he was writing, but, in Tom-like fashion, he also encouraged me to write my own essay on this subject. In his essay, Tom writes that I stuck a fat Penguin Classic into his hand, saying, "Look. Pablo Neruda!" Only now, after reading his version of what happened, has it occurred to me that Tom did not want this book that I so heartily offered, mainly because he had even less bookshelf space in his Copenhagen apartment than I had in my tiny American bungalow. But when he saw that the book was by Neruda, he couldn't resist. An avid Neruda fan, he'd recently made a pilgrimage to the poet's home, Isla Negra, which now serves as an archive holding every imaginable relic of Neruda's personal and literary life. Tom had never seen the book I was trying to give him in the Neruda archives at Isla Negra. He'd never even known it existed. A memoir Neruda had been editing when he died in 1973, the book recounts his childhood, his travels, his flight from the Chilean police, his exile and life as a poet. In his essay, Tom writes that he kept the Neruda memoir I gave him, jotting down a single line from this book about the torture and death of a Santiago poet in 1920, Jose Domingo Gomez

Rojas. Tom saved this line about the tortured and murdered poet on a scrap of paper. He tried to locate the poetry of Rojas, but couldn't find an English translation.

Around the time he discovered the poet, Roja, in the Neruda memoir, Tom's job with the Danish Medical Association required him to translate into English the first psychiatric treatment manual for torture survivors, a Danish publication used by the Torture Rehabilitation Center in Copenhagen. The work required him to read graphic case studies about torture victims. He said these "tales of torment inflicted on human beings by other human beings" made him feel damaged to the point of needing to unburden himself in some way. He wrote a short story about a fictional Latin American torture survivor, a poet bearing a strong resemblance to the Santiago poet, Rojas. Then he wrote a second story on this subject. But the character and the story still weren't done with him yet. In 2002, he began a novel that opens with an image of a Chilean poet named Bernardo Greene. Outcast and hopelessly damaged by torture inflicted by his own government, he sits in a street-side café in Copenhagen on a chill June day. "How much of a survivor, in fact, survives?" Bernardo muses. "How much must remain of a survivor for him also to be called a man?"

Tom's book, *In the Company of Angels*, is a wise, beautiful novel that is now enjoying publication in Europe and the U.S. It's a contemporary work that I already count as great literature, and it blessedly continues to survive in this ever-changing publishing climate. As I sit here on this end-of-summer day, listening to the cicadas churn as loudly as they did the morning I trekked south to rescue those books from burning, I contemplate all the great print books that are rapidly disappearing from our lives, and I feel damaged. It seems that there is an almost mystical thread that connects the survival of a man with the survival of the printed word. Surely the torturing of a human being is a much more savage crime than book burning, but the bureaucratic impulse that nearly led to the burning of those 5,000 books is the same impulse that allows despotic leaders to deny, and often hide, even greater crimes that dehumanize us as individuals and as a culture. The destruction of human flesh, and the destruction of the flesh made word by books, are both acts of savagery.

Good writers are part archivists, part guardian angels. They safe-guard us by recalling and imagining stories about people, baring truths that the faint-hearted turn away from, and that the purely evil try to hide. Great writing also evolves from the reading of great books, as Tom's novel evolved from reading Neruda's memoir and from re-imagining the tragic figure of the lesser-known poet, Rojas. So now that I've been nudged gently into writing about this subject, I return to the questions asked by the torture survivor who haunts the pages of a book that arose in the mind of a fiction writer as he read a great poet's book that survived bureaucratic whim and fire. There are those who would say that literature will survive, but in a different form, and I heartily applaud the writers, editors, and publishers who are transitioning gracefully into other forms of publication so that literature will endure. I am in awe of librarians who continue to create free literacy programs for every member of our communities, despite the continuous cuts to their yearly budgets. Still, I wonder. If the printed book disappears from our daily lives, if we can't hold a book in our hands and savor it page by page, how much of ourselves will survive, and how much of ourselves will remain wholly human?

The Plain of Sorrento

"And placing his hand on mine, with a cheerful countenance that comforted me, he led me into the secret things."

–Dante Alighieri, *Inferno*

I

A BRIEF AND VIOLENT AFTERNOON STORM blew through the Gulf of Naples an hour earlier, shredding the January sky. Sitting on the roof of a cliff-top hotel in Piano di Sorrento after the rain, I looked out at the fine threads of gray clouds, patches of raw pink, the pale fog that camouflaged Mount Vesuvius across the bay. Down in the Marina di Cassano, fine white-caps scribbled across the deep lapis water while seagulls unfolded like handkerchiefs above yellow fishing boats floating beside piers made of lava rocks. At first, I believed I was too high up to smell the salt and fish. Then a temperamental wind swept in the smell of brine. I looked around, relieved to find that the only way to this spot was through my room's window or by breaking the glass in the emergency exit door that led to a hidden stairwell. I felt remote, but I wasn't ready to share this lonely view with just anyone.

Rising from the single lounge chair on the roof's edge, I dodged dirty puddles, overturned pots of cactuses on the rain-swept tiles, climbed over the concrete wall onto my balcony and stepped back into my room. I called home to hear my husband's voice. Though he stopped singing long before I met him, Rick remains a baritone, slightly rough edged from the occasional cigar, reassuringly pitched as he explained that Berlusconi was in Washington, supporting military action against Iraq. It had snowed eight inches in South Carolina, and there was a large possum living in our backyard. My husband had rented a castle in Scotland.

"It's more affordable than renting a place at the beach," he said.

I imagined him sitting at the picnic table on our back porch, beside the red camellia blooming in the snow, a glass of Bowmore Scotch and The National Trust Handbook at his elbow, while he waited for the possum to crawl into the trap he'd rigged with bacon in the garden shed. Blind in his right eye, he looked with his left eye through a magnifying glass at the small print in the handbook, browsing through pictures of thatched roof cottages, gothic churches transformed into bed and breakfasts.

His sight loss had made us both urgent travelers. In the years since it began, we'd booked overseas flights with six layovers, stayed at hotels for off-season rates on the outskirts of the famous cities we'd always wanted to see. We differed only in our choice of destinations. He preferred cold, mountainous regions, the geography of his Virginia childhood; I was happiest in warm places surrounded by water. So when I took a teaching assignment traveling through Italy with fourteen college students and an Italian language professor, he said he'd rather stay home, save up for a trip to Scotland.

After talking for almost an hour, I hung up the phone and reopened the casement window. The sky had mended, darkened, and a soft rain fell across the black water. Naples burned like a strand of red and yellow bonfires, orange smoke rising from them into the mist. I closed the window, feeling a lovesick pang for the late afternoon view of the bay.

II

All through Tuscany, I'd felt landlocked. We were living outside the town of Tarantela, below Cortona, in an eleventh-century villa that once served as a leper colony. The villa's current owner was an American painter from our small Carolina town, a former student of the private women's college where I taught journalism and creative writing. After the painter's husband was shot by the man he caught embezzling from him, she'd fled to Italy, bought and restored the villa while recovering from his death. She whitewashed the stone walls and polished the high walnut ceiling beams. She covered the terra cotta floors with sheep skin rugs. She filled its labyrinth of cell-like rooms and wide hallways with heavy antique chairs, couches upholstered with wine red fabric. She wove dried flowers into stacks of olive wood inside the drafty fireplaces and installed small heaters that puffed out frail air beneath the casement windows of each room. Even after we turned all the heaters on, a chill remained inside the painter's house, so we all wore the white bathrobes she provided for each of her guests over our jeans and sweaters while we slept.

Her paintings from this recovery period hung throughout the villa, each a testament to a different stage of her grief. A picture of a bare, arthritic olive tree on a golden hill hung in the library; in the kitchen above the work table, she'd hung a dark oil of a ripe pomegranate, its red flesh split in half, its black seeds exposed. In the master bedroom, there was a nude. Pale-skinned and womanly, she stood facing away from the viewer, her left arm bent across her chest as she reached behind her shoulder to clasp her long, auburn hair at the base of her neck. I felt in awe of the painter's ability to rise after her husband's death, to turn away from her own sinking grief. She'd given us free use of the villa for the entire week. Despite her astonishing generosity, I felt uneasy inside her cold, voluptuous house.

From the villa, we took day trips to the medieval hill towns of Siena and Assisi, visiting the homes of the most austere saints. In Siena, we headed straight for Saint Catherine's Sanctuary. A gentle breeze blew up through the medieval alleys hung with clean laundry, creating a hush in the open, whitewashed entryway. A soapstone statue of Saint Catherine with pink geraniums at her feet guarded over the heavy chapel door. Inside, the chapel was small, warm, and feminine. Neatly pressed lace covered the altar; pots of white lilies lined up along the butter-yellow marble aisles. Someone played the violin in the sacristy. We all filed into the first pew, sat, and listened.

Raised Catholic, I was schooled by nuns in the lives of the mystics. I grew up measuring out each season according to their feast days. Every year, on the day after Halloween, my classmates and I dressed up like our patron saints. I was assigned Saint Anne. Wrapped in one of my mother's worn bed sheets, cinched at the waist with twine, I paraded around the classroom with girls dressed like women martyrs--Lucy, Theresa, and Agnes. When it was my turn to read from my index card in front of the class, I recited, "Saint Anne was very old and could not have children, so she prayed beneath a laurel bush until an angel of the Lord appeared and told her she would become the mother of our Lady. She is the patron saint of cabinet makers and housewives."

How I longed to change my name to Catherine in those days, to speak of heroic Catherine of Siena's physical trials, her long ecstasies and exquisite visions. At sixteen, she cut off her luxurious golden hair and refused to marry. When her mother took her to a spa at Vignone with hopes of preparing her for marriage, Catherine scalded herself at the source of the hot springs and exposed herself to the small pox so that no man would want her. Shorn of her lovely hair, scalded, and scarred from small pox scabs, she was allowed to enter the Third Order of the Dominican Sisters of Penance. For three years, she secluded herself. She went only to Mass, broke silence only for confession, and sustained herself only on the Blessed Sacrament. She was seen levitating while in prayer, and when she took Communion the Host was seen shivering and flying into her mouth on its own. Then she gave up the beloved seclusion of the cloister to go out among the sick and sinful. She once befriended a condemned man who'd found God just days before the date of his execution. She knelt beside him as he waited for the guillotine's blade to drop, listening to his final words, "Jesus and Catherine." She caught his severed head before it could roll into the basket.

Growing up, I never questioned such stories. I accepted, somewhat dimly, the notion that suffering and giving oneself completely to another's loss were acts that made a woman most worthy. Sitting in the wooden pew in front of Saint Catherine's church, listening to the violin, I knew that I'd outgrown my girlhood romance with glamorous acts of devotion. Catherine's ascetics now seemed reckless, selfish. How dare she ravage her young, healthy body? How dare she put her mother through such intolerable worry over her well-being? I did feel the profound comfort of the violin's music, but I wondered if such calm had been earned through Saint Catherine's suffering or if this were simply a matter of immaculate housekeeping. It was possible, I thought, to live inside this warm and tidy church. The students felt this too. Many of them were Baptists, some traveling for the first time out of South Carolina, but they all lingered by the altar, unable to leave. As they knelt and prayed, a tiny nun, her veil tucked inside a down ski jacket, bustled up the aisle, her arms filled with a grocery sack of cheese, bread, and lettuce. She entered the sacristy, the music stopped, and the church filled with practical silence. Standing to leave, I imagined the nun urging a starving, ethereal violinist to eat, please eat, God's music can wait.

We broke for lunch. In a cafe overlooking the Piazza del Campo, where horsemen race barebacked in the Palio every summer, the Italian professor and I talked over full plates of panini, pan forte, and almond cookies.

"You and I both have the souls of pilgrims," my colleague declared suddenly. "We both love searching for wonder. Both of us are relatively lost."

I'd never thought of myself as a pilgrim before, but the idea puzzled and appealed to me. "Why do people go on pilgrimages?"

She paused, considering. "I once met a woman in Austria who was on a pilgrimage because she felt guilty."

"What was she doing? "

My colleague shrugged. "I guess you had to see her. It was like she was atoning for something, or leaving it behind."

Sitting in that café overlooking a piazza that spread like a wide and shallow brown bowl, I felt extremely happy, and healthy. I had no idea what time it was or where we were going next, and I didn't care. At the same time, I felt a steady undercurrent of guilty dread. It was the first trip I'd taken alone since my husband had begun losing his sight. I wished I'd tried harder to convince him to come with me, to see all the lovely and mysterious places I was seeing. Yes, I agreed, I suppose we were a little like pilgrims.

In Assisi, we took taxis up to the entrance of the Prisons' Hermitage of St. Francis. We hiked the quiet, sloping path up Mount Subasio, through the forest of pines, past the ancient live oak where St. Francis once preached to the birds. There were no monks about when we reached the stone entryway, only a dry well topped with stones and purple phlox blooming mysteriously in the dead of winter, so we took ourselves through the monastery.

The disciples of Saint Francis humbled themselves by building low doorways. As we stooped beneath the doorframes and climbed through dark and narrow stone halls, my stomach cramped from the tight spaces, and I had no idea what I was seeing. When we reached daylight on the other side of the hermitage and saw the two fat, white doves perched above the exit sign, flying in and out of a high open window, I was tremendously relieved.

"You must see the grottoes," my colleague insisted. "It's the only way that you will understand how Saint Francis lived, how much of the world he gave up for his beliefs."

The paths leading through the grottoes were lined with life-sized statues of monks posed in their favorite activities. One crouched on a low stone, his hand outstretched as though to shield his averted eyes. The other stood on a higher rock, his hand outstretched in the same direction, but he was facing whatever revealed itself to him. A statue of Saint Francis lay on the ground with his bare feet crossed as he stargazed. We walked up to a higher path and found one of the grottoes, a low cave where a hermit could immure himself, denying light and sound and movement for months, sometimes years.

The students asked how the hermits ate, drank, defecated. Who took care of them while they were becoming saints?

"The other monks built a wall of stones up over the entrance to keep him inside," my colleague said. "They took a stone out and passed the food and water through the hole. They passed everything out the same way."

The students asked if women ever lived here, and what about Saint Clare?

"Clare and Francis were lovers," my colleague declared.

I had come to Saint Clare as an adult, and I'd often thought her fierce devotion to Saint Francis was both destructive and erotic, but I'd never heard this version of the story before. At eighteen, Clare came down from her family's home on Mt. Subasio to watch Francis preach the Lenten course in the church of San Giorgio at Assisi. She was so inspired by him she ran away from her father's house that night to the Portiuncula, where Francis met her with a candle in his hand. She took off her rich gown for him, let him dress her in a rough tunic and thick veil. He cut her hair. Then he established her in the poor chapel of San Damiano, where she remained at his insistence, largely against her own will, for the next forty years of her life.

Like Saint Catherine, she practiced austerities that wrecked her body. She wore no stockings or sandals in winter. She slept on the ground, starved herself, and wore a hair shirt next to her skin. She was the servant of servants, known to wash the feet of her lay-sisters when they returned from begging, to stay up late at night to tuck in the younger nuns who tossed off their covers in sleep. Only Saint Francis could convince her to eat, to sleep. He once pleaded with her, "Our bodies are not of brass and our strength is not the strength of stone." Blind and ill from his own austerities, he returned to her at the end of his life, and she erected a hut for him in an olive grove so that he could compose "The Canticle of the Sun." After his death, as the procession that carried his remains passed San Domiano, Saint Clare came out to kiss the stigmata on his hands and feet.

Perhaps my colleague's statement disturbed me because it was partly true. Clare and Francis were married in every sense of the word but the body. If they weren't lovers, they certainly should have been. Still, I felt uneasy with this story's lesson. How much, realistically, should a wife give up for her husband? How much of his suffering should she bear? Beside the grotto, one of the students found a slip of paper tucked under a rock, an unfinished prayer that read simply, "Dear God." Standing on the side of the mountain, the harsh wind cutting through my wool coat and two sweaters, I watched the students patiently take notes and shiver in the icy wind. I wondered why we'd brought them to such a cold, desperate place. Would they recognize that women needn't sacrifice themselves completely to be worthy? Did they have better role models back home, women with whom they could study grace? Dear God, I thought as I walked down the mountain to meet our taxis.

The following day was a Sunday, our only day off from visiting churches. The students were to read, write in their journals, finish their laundry. I made a frittata with pecorino and last season's zucchini from the villa's freezer. I poured blood orange juice and toasted thick slices of Tuscan bread, spreading them with wild truffle and rabbit pate. Then I went out to sit at a picnic table behind the villa, between the swimming pool covered with a black tarp and the young grape arbor asleep beneath the dead, gold grass.

I'd been reading Dante's *Inferno* with hopes of improving my Italian. But for days I had been stuck at the gates of hell, nodding off to sleep when I reached the passage about the neutral angels and the blind souls who lived without blame or praise. That afternoon was no different. When I reached the unfortunates who were never alive, I dozed, dropping the book, losing my place. I was tired of lost souls, frustrated with the mystics and their reckless austerities. If Saint Francis truly believed our bodies weren't made of brass, why hadn't he taken better care of himself? Who had he thought would attend him while he suffered to become a saint? Had Clare ever doubted her ability to take care of him?

The year before, while I planned this trip, a blood clot lodged itself into the central artery of my husband's right eye. In the unreal days following this sudden blindness, while we searched for a reason, the doctors speculated out loud, blaming a brain tumor, multiple sclerosis and then, finally, his heart. One day, I sat in a dark room of a cardiac center, watching a nurse rub a Vaseline-covered Doplar over his chest. Cold sweating beneath the pile of our winter coats in my lap, I looked rudely into my husband's body as the nurse traced his carotid artery, his heart clenching inside his chest. When she reached his waist, I thought I saw a fetus, floating blind and sexless inside his abdomen.

I fled the room to go sit outside in our truck. After the nurse finished with him, my husband slid into the passenger seat, shaking his head.

"I never thought I'd see the day when another woman rubbed Vaseline all over my body while my wife watched," he said.

"I saw a baby in your stomach," I said.

My husband frowned. Then he took my hand. "You've got to pull yourself together. You can't go around seeing babies in my stomach and running out of the doctor's office."

"What am I supposed to see? What am I supposed to do?"

"We go on as though none of this has happened."

The doctor finally declared that my husband was afflicted with "dumb luck." The blood clot had shot from a tiny hole in his heart straight into the central artery of his right eye, and there was no way of knowing if this would happen to the left one. We didn't allow ourselves to speculate about where the first clot might have landed, a prospect that sent me down a trail of thoughts darker than any form of blindness. Instead, we bought a tiny pillbox with the days of the weeks labeled on it for his blood thinners and put an eye chart on our refrigerator door for him to test his sight. My husband kept his near blindness to himself, but when he thought I wasn't looking he passed his hand over his good eye while squinting at the eye chart on the fridge to see if any of his vision had returned. Once, when I caught him doing this, I placed my own hand over his good eye and asked him what he saw when he looked at me.

"I see the top of your head, the bottom of your chin. The rest of your face is missing." I dropped my hand, he turned away, and we never played this game again.

The winter morning I read Dante out behind the Tuscan villa, I began feeling the familiar suspension of hospital waiting rooms, the dread that had dulled my senses since the beginning of my husband's blindness. In his book *A Grief Observed*, C.S. Lewis writes, "No one ever told me that grief felt so like fear." Over the last months, I'd begun to understand this. I felt the same sinking of the stomach, the same restlessness, but I felt guilty too because I wasn't the one suffering from the loss. It wasn't mine, but as I watched it happen to him, waiting without blame or praise, I felt as though it had become my own. I knew I could disappear beneath the weight of it. I also knew that by taking on my husband's grief, I wasn't much consolation to him. I wanted him here with me. At the same time I wanted to be far away from his loss, if just for a little while, so that I could go home restored and brave again, a steady source of comfort to him.

That had been my plan, but even now, after touring the birthplace of my most heroic saints, I seriously wondered if it were possible to remain devoted to another's suffering without losing sight of oneself completely. Reading Dante, I understood the torments of inertia much too clearly; the only way to fight it was to keep moving. I put the Inferno in my coat pocket and went hiking along the muddy Etruscan road bordered by wild asparagus and rosemary, into the silver olive groves.

III

As I sat inside the clifftop hotel room in Piano di Sorrento, the plain that overlooks the more famous town of Sorrento, Tuscany seemed like a fever dream of medieval hill towns muted by frost, blue laurel, groves of silver olive trees. Worn out from the long bus ride south, the students and my colleague slept in their own rooms. I remained awake, thinking of how deceptive illness can be, of how its terrifying constraints can make any journey feel exalted. Having descended from the cold, mystic regions of Umbria and Tuscany, I felt both let down and free to contemplate all the wonders I'd witnessed in Italy.

I made a random list: Roman boys played baseball in the third century; Saint Peter's Basilica is 600 feet long and 450 feet high; Boticelli's Annunciation; Caravaggio's Medusa; when Giotto was a boy, he painted flies so real that his master Cimbue thought they were alive and tried to shoo them off the canvas. My mind glutted with wonders, my body pleasantly reduced to living by sight, taste and touch, I began itemizing the smaller acts of faith that I'd truly understood on this trip: the taste of blood oranges; finding my way from the Colosseum to Trastevere in Rome without a map; a hot shower in a private hotel room; this view of the Bay of Naples.

I no longer felt like a pilgrim. I wished I'd brought my copy of The Odyssey instead of Inferno. Searching the bay, I looked for the Sirenuse Islands, where Odysseus chained himself to the mast of his ship, stuffed wax into his crew members' ears to mute out the sweet siren song. But it was too dark to see anything. The twilight rain had driven the staff inside the hotel, and they had gathered down in the lobby to play cards. The clink of their poker chips, laughter, and hoarse voices rose up the stairway to my room. I went downstairs in search of change for postcard stamps, a cup for brushing my teeth.

Across from the front desk, burly Sorrentine men were seated around a wide round table, hunched over hands of cards. Tall and unshaven, their southern accents were unfamiliar, daunting. I decided to approach the oldest one. Straight-backed and hazel-eyed, his olive skin was ashy, his thin white hair carefully combed over his forehead. His husky voice and sleight-of-hand card shuffling reminded me of my Uncle Gus, from the Sicilian side of my family.

"What game are you playing?" I asked. The men all stopped playing, and stared.

"Poker," the oldest one said.

"Do you have change for a twenty?" He must have liked the looks of me too because he grasped my hand, stood and wrapped his other arm gently around my waist. I couldn't help but lean slightly into his chest as he wheeled me around the table while each younger man stood, nodded, reached deep into his pocket for a fist-sized wad of cash. One by one, they shook their heads, "No, nothing small enough to break a twenty."

The housekeeper walked over to the table, a beige poodle at her heels. She pulled a slender pile of bills from her dress pocket, counted out the exact change, and took my twenty. She gave me two postcard stamps, which slipped from my hand. The dog pounced and ate the stamps off the floor, snapping at my fingers as I tried to save them.

"Briciola!" the housekeeper cried, pulling the dog away too late, ordering her back behind the front desk. I looked down at the damp spot on the floor where the stamps had been devoured. The housekeeper shrugged apologetically. I asked for a glass to take back to my room, but she shook her head firmly, "No glass in the rooms." She pulled a stack of plastic cups from behind the bamboo bar beside the table. "Use these." Then she nodded toward the old man. "It's okay to talk to Lozario. He's family. His wife died, so he comes here to sit in the lobby, to play cards with his nephews."

The poker game had ended. Chips and cards were scattered across the pale blue tablecloth, the nephews gone up to the mezzanine floor to watch the news on the t.v. Lozario went behind the bar, brought out a green, unlabeled bottle of red wine and pulled out a chair for me to sit next to him at the table. He separated my two plastic toothbrush cups, filled them both with the dark wine. I watched helplessly, wondering how I could get my hands on more clean cups, eyeing the poodle that had curled up in a worn, floral chair beside the front desk. It was still whimpering and snarling.

"That dog is afraid," Lozario said, nodding toward the front door, the black street outside the glass. "There is something out there she fears. She is telling us she wants our protection."

"What is her name again?" I asked.

"Briciola. It means 'crumb.'"

He cut, I dealt the cards, and we began a wild yet familiar game of poker, a cross between five card draw and Texas Hold 'em. Three students wandered into the lobby. Many times during the trip, I'd admired their poise. They'd walked up the side of a cold mountain without complaining. They'd negotiated the twisted, dreamlike streets of Rome without knowing a word of Italian. They'd been stealing up to me, one-by-one, confiding moments of solace or understanding they'd experienced during this long, physically demanding trip. "I climbed to the top of Giotto's bell tower and saw all of Florence," one confided. "I thought I was having a heart attack from climbing all those steps, but it was like nothing I've ever seen." Another claimed that after the hermitage in Assisi, she'd fallen asleep and seen a glowing cross above the foot of her bed.

I was truly glad my fellow travelers were having good visions, happy they'd been given what they needed to see, but I didn't recall having this confident bearing or understanding when I was their age. I wondered if grace came naturally to them, or if they were just better at pretending to be courageous. They had visited a Sicilian barber in Cortona, but during the long bus ride down to Piano di Sorrento, they'd pulled their stylish haircuts into ponytails and wiped all the makeup from their faces. They looked almost thirteen as they smiled and eagerly joined the game. We tossed Euro cents and almonds along with the poker chips into the pot. We taught Lozario how to say, "one-eyed jack" and "suicide king" in English. At one point, I counted only thirty-two cards in the deck. Emptying Lozario's black velvet game bag onto the table, I found two more decks of thirty-two cards, more poker chips, and we used those too. Somehow, the number of cards had become unimportant. I'd stopped worrying about clean cups and lost postcard stamps. Lozario's young wine was fruity, alive on the tongue, and it eased my shyness. Speaking Italian sprinkled with English, some French, and a lot of hand gestures, we talked about the impending war until Lozario softly grabbed my hands, "Please. No more. No more talk of politics," he said. We kept talking. It was the talk we both wanted anyway.

"Do you have a boyfriend in South Carolina?" Lozario asked.

"I'm married," I said. "Eleven years."

I looked at the gold wedding band on his left hand, afraid to ask about his wife, but he offered, "My wife died of cancer. It was so bad. At the end, I couldn't watch." He nodded up toward the nephews on the mezzanine floor. "It helps me to come here, to play cards with them."

I wanted to tell him that the gravely ill are much braver than those who must watch them. I wanted to tell him that I once ran out of the room while my husband was having a cardiogram because I'd seen places in his body that a wife isn't intended to see. I didn't know the Italian word for stoicism, so I dealt another hand.

"Where did you go before you were here?" Lozario asked.

"Umbria and Tuscany," I said. "We went to the homes of Saint Catherine and Saint Francis."

"The saints are for grandmothers and children," he said bitterly. He topped off my wine and set the empty bottle on the table. "You are all proper girls with many manners. Finish your wine. It is time for you to go back to your rooms."

Returning to my room, I was amazed by Lozario's ability to make everything--even my pocket full of loose change and the wine-stained cup I now carried--feel consoling. Dozing in bed, I listened to the hotel creak in the wind, the pipes clanging inside the walls. I imagined the noisy Sorrentines climbing up the pipes, hammering on them. All night, I heard their friendly, industrious noises in my sleep.

IV

When I stepped onto my balcony the next morning, Lozario and one of his nephews were on the roof, threading a black cable through the ceiling beams of the unfinished hotel wing. On the street below, two Fiats had collided on a downhill curve. Two carabinieri were parked behind the wreck on the high, treacherous curb, negotiating loudly with the accident victims.

"Ciao, bella," Lozario called out. "Where are you going today?"

"Positano," I called back. "But I have the morning free. What's the easiest way to walk to Sorrento?"

Lozario looked confused by my question, so I repeated it.

"It is too far to walk," he said firmly. "You must take the train."

"But if I wanted to walk to Sorrento, which way would I need to turn when I leave the hotel?"

Lozario shook his head, began climbing down the ladder. "You turn right."

Throughout the trip, I had been telling my students to take walks at different times of the day, to talk to people. "Go roaming," I told them. "But use common sense. Don't put yourselves in any danger." Hotel map of the city in hand, I intended to follow my own advice. Turning right on the Via Ripa di Cassano, I followed the cliffs and umbrella pines overlooking the marina, hoping to scout out the city, find the train station. The sidewalks were lined by groves of blood orange and lemon trees, their full limbs hanging over high stucco walls, dropping fruit onto the wet pavement. I wanted to pull a blood orange down from a tree, then I thought better of it.

The street cleaners in green jump suits were out, rolling the fallen fruit to the curb with their stick brooms, mildly watching everything. I lost track of the signs for the train station and Sorrento. Keeping an eye on the cliffs so that I wouldn't get too confused, I turned left, then left again, onto a narrow side street that led to Saint Michael the Archangel church. Just before the church, I ducked into an open doorway beside a sign that read, "Visitate Il Presepe del Nuova Millennia. I Ragazzi del Presepe." I stepped down into a dark, small room that smelled of river rocks and found a nativity.

It was an entire Italian village, complete with a chestnut vendor, a butcher, a weaver and a produce stand filled with bushel baskets of peppers, wine, bread and salami. A tiny bonfire flickered beneath a caldron of boiling water in front of the tiny Arrotino Inn. A medieval castle sat on top of a high cliff spotted with lambs. The village inhabitants were finely detailed, their hard lives chiseled into their faces; the washerwoman wringing a white towel had a goiter on her neck. Only the Christ Child was idealized. The blond, blue-eyed baby slept in a porcelain pillbox instead of a manger, gold-swathed angels leaning over him. Shepherds with lambs wrapped around their shoulders shaded their eyes to gaze at him.

I must have stayed for a half hour before I noticed the light. When I'd first entered the nativity, the village had been dark, its details visible only by the orange bonfires and the torches beside the tiny inn. Now the afternoon light was turning to violet. Soon, the bonfires and torches ignited again. On a wooden platform above me, a man sat in darkness before a glowing t.v. screen, watching over the nativity. I nodded to him and stood through another dawn, another afternoon, twilight and nightfall. The complete rotation of the earth on its axis took ten minutes, ending when the strains of "Jesu, Joy of Man's Desiring" cut off and the overhead lights went on. Charmed, disappointed, I fished coins out of my change purse, tossed them into the collection basket, and returned to the hotel.

An hour later, the tour bus crawled along the Amalfi Drive, teetering hundreds of feet above the coast. The Roman bus driver played a bluegrass CD on the radio while he negotiated the narrow coastal road, and the students sang, dancing in the aisle. At our first glimpse of Positano, the students stopped dancing, and someone behind me murmured, "It's like we're hanging off the side of heaven." The guide coached the bus driver around the increasingly tight curves, saying, "Piano, piano."

In this context, the word "piano" means to go slowly, gently, carefully. That afternoon, as I looked over the harsh precipice at the surreal and lovely hill town, it occurred to me that this was the only way to approach the inconceivable, both violent loss and the mysteriously holy, without becoming completely lost. The town's hotels and houses clung to the side of a cliff, half of them covered in shadow, the other half bleached white by the sun. From a distance, they looked like stones in an ancient stadium. Hundreds of feet below on the shore of the Tyrrhenian Sea, the aquamarine water frothed against the sand.

The bus stopped completely beside an overlook, and we left our winter coats on our seats. Out on the road, the students gently declined all offers to see the yellow Moorish church. As they followed me, I marveled at how trusting they seemed. I didn't know the path down to the marina. I knew only that I was going down to the sea. Passing a dark statue of Saint Francis in a private garden, we descended hundreds of stone steps bordered by walls hung with bougainvillea and caper bushes. We walked beside cliffside rooftops stacked high with trumpet vine. We continued down into the deserted, stone market place just above the beach, where tall, thin cactuses grew from rocks and wrought iron flowers climbed the glass doors of the closed boutiques. The students caught sight of the beach and walked ahead while I lingered briefly to discuss our evening plans in Sorrento with the guide. After he went off to make phone calls, I found the girls pacing the shore, bending over, searching. Moving closer, I realized that there was no sand. The fishing boats were dry docked on brown, smooth rocks.

"What did you lose?" I asked one of the students.

"Nothing," she said. "We found these."

The local masons had thrown their broken tiles into the ocean, and the water had polished them into smooth terra cotta stones, coughing them back onto the shore where they mingled like dull rubies and jade among the brown rocks. I joined the students, filling my pockets with the painted stones. I found two that could have been from a child's nursery, a clown's elbow, a pointed hat. Pockets full, the students began filling their backpacks while storm clouds simmered between the cliffs above the town. One of the students took her umbrella from its case and used it as a bag for her finds. It made no sense at all to fill our pockets with rocks; we had to climb hundreds of steps at the end of the afternoon. Giddy, overwhelmed by this preternatural landscape, I felt the stones clank reassuringly in my hands. I spotted the Sirenuse Islands out in the Tyrrhenian Sea, gray and smoky in the distance.   Two of the students took off their shoes, and waded into the calm waves. They were fearless as they walked into the water.

Hell Broth and Poisoned Entrails: An Affair with Scottish Cookery

ONE APRIL, RICK, HUNTER, AND I LIVED in a flat in Old Town Edinburgh, on the Royal Mile, across from the World's End Close, an alley named so because it was once the very edge of the original town, and therefore, the very edge of the world to the town's original inhabitants. Along a street lined with whiskey shops, and up three flights of stairs, we found our flat called "The Story Teller's Apartment." Freshly painted white, its bedroom was filled with a high, soft bed and a window seat overlooking a bright blue pub called "The World's End." Our landlady, Fiona, had left us a hand-typed list of sites and amenities called "Fiona's Favorites," which read, "There's a wee shop on the corner where you can buy groceries. If it's whiskey you're after, I'd suggest the Royal Mile Whiskies."

Rick was unpacking his suitcase, folding sweaters into a pine chest in the bedroom. I knew he was plotting a trip to those whisky shops. I had only a dim notion of what I was after. As Edinburgh's native son, the writer Robert Louis Stevenson, once wrote, "The great affair of travel is to move; to feel the needs and hitches of our own life more nearly; to come down off this feather-bed of civilization, and find the globe granite underfoot and strewn with cutting stone." I skimmed down "Fiona's Favorites" until I found a listing for "The Real Mary King's Close: An Historically Accurate Interpretation of 16th through 19th century Edinburgh. Witness the highs and lows of sixteenth-century townhouses. Visit the home of a grave digger's family to discover the truth about how the Burgh council dealt with the plague of 1645." I reread the words, "plague" and "grave digger," knowing only that I wanted to move deeper into the cold, cut stone of one of Europe's most storied cities.

"This looks really good," I said. "You want to go here first?"

"I've always wanted to see that," Rick said.

We walked up the street to "The Real Mary King's Close" and booked a tour for the next morning. While in the gift shop, we picked up a free membership to The Friends of the Classic Malts Club, receiving a flavor map of Scottish whiskies. My husband prefers the island malts, the heavily-peated ones hinting of ocean brine. He likes feeling as if he's swallowing a bonfire while sipping whisky, tasting the ashes of an ancient hearth at the back of his throat. Though not a whisky drinker, I enjoy watching Rick take pleasure in his favorite drink, this Scottish "water of life." I followed him gamely in and out of the whisky shops along the Royal Mile, making friends with the shopkeepers who poured generous samples of any whiskey we wanted into drams, saying, "Give this one a nose. Then take a wee taste and let it warm the back of your throat."

Around the fourth shop, I discovered a whisky I actually liked, a lower highland malt called Auchentoshan. The color of honey, it tasted of heather and pears. Its heat was as mellow as evening sunlight. Warmed by my newfound fondness for lowland whisky, my husband proudly bought me my own ladylike bottle of twelve-year-old Auchentoshan, 750 milliters to take back to the Story Teller's Apartment and drink.

All our fifteen-year-old son wanted to do that day was eat. Fearless as his name, Hunter would eat haggis for breakfast, lunch, and dinner if we had regular access to it, never mind that this dish is made from a sheep's heart, liver, and lungs minced together, mixed with onion and oatmeal, and stuffed into the sheep's plucked stomach. After whisky shopping, we took Hunter down to the farmers market behind Edinburgh Castle and bought him a bag of Scotch eggs—boiled eggs dipped in beaten egg, rolled in mace-seasoned sausage, dipped again in more beaten egg, then deep fried. We bought a black-faced sheep and mustard pie, links of blood sausage, homemade short bread. On our way back to the Story Teller's Apartment, we stopped at a cheesemonger's shop for a wedge of Lanark Blue Cheese, mould-ripened and made from unpasteurized ewes' milk.

None of these traditional foods taste bad; my difficulty with Scottish cookery is that these dishes were developed for heartier appetites of roving clan members, the strong stomachs of farm hands who cooked lamb and grains together in iron pots over open fires after a day spent harvesting five hundred bales of hay. An Italian American accustomed to fish, pasta and olive oil, I usually sip the Scotch broth and head straight for the safety of shortbread when in Scotland.

That evening, my twelve-year-old lowland whisky opened up with a drop of water and revealed the pleasures of minced organ meats, making everything go down quite easily. Sipping whisky from a coffee cup, I ate the unpasteurized cheese, a Scotch egg, a slice of sheep pie, the haggis, and cullen skink, (fish, potato and onion soup). Savoring a finger of shortbread with one last cup of whisky, I had several revelations: Collops in a pan were really just a variation of the Italian peasant dish, osso bucco. A clootie dumpling was quite similar to an Italian panna cotta. Finally, I determined that Scottish cooking, inspired by French cooking, must have been born of Italian chefs 200 years ago.

I fell asleep early that night, but I awoke sweating at 10 p.m., throat burning from flames that must have lain dormant beneath that sweet lowland whisky. My head and heart pounded to the sound of late-night patrons stumbling out of the World's End Pub across the street. I'd slept hard, with my left arm bent oddly beneath me, and now it hung numb and heavy at my side. Not wanting to wake Rick or Hunter, I decided to sit on the window seat and read myself back to sleep by the glow of the street lamp. I pulled down one of the books from Fiona's bookshelf, The Town Below the Ground, and opened it to a chapter about the plague victims of Mary King's Close.

According to this book, the plague of 1645 spread quickly by fleas that fed off infected rats. The inhabitants of Mary King's Close who suffered from the plague were sealed inside their own houses, a red cross and the words, "God have Mercy," painted across their doors. Two months later, when the city council felt it safe to remove the bodies, rigor mortis had taken hold. Death cart laborers dismembered the corpses with axes and hauled the remains away in any kind of improvised shroud.

I shut the book, feeling strange hitches in my body, my abdomen cinched too tightly to my esophagus, my heart, liver, and lungs surely poisoned by the diseased organs of the countless Scottish farm animals I'd eaten a few hours before. A needling fire had risen up my deadened left arm, stiffening my neck, fevering my pounding head. I ran to the bathroom and looked in the mirror, saw what looked like a plague victim -- blotchy skin, witchy hair, tiny broken blood vessels in eyes gritty in their sockets. I went back to the window seat, opened *The Town Below the Ground*, and read about Bubonic plague symptoms: fever, head and muscle ache, abdominal pain, thirst, delirium, a stiff neck, and an intense desire to sleep, which, if yielded to, quickly proved fatal. I read about the infamous buboes, tender nodes growing in the underarms and necks of the plague victims, ranging from one to ten centimeters in size. I did not have any buboes. I lay back on the soft tartan bed, dizzily relieved. God have Mercy, I thought. Slowly, slowly, near dawn, I yielded to sleep.

The next morning, I awoke free of muscle ache and fever, but shaky and swollen, my stomach as changeable as Scottish spring weather. During the ten-minute walk to Mary King's Close, we witnessed white mist, chill drizzle, clouds threading and scudding across a round, brilliant sun holding itself just above the pointiest spire of Saint Giles Cathedral. These inclement feelings lingered within me at the tour entrance. We were greeted by a college kid dressed up in period costume. He introduced himself as a plague cleaner, and took us down into his home, a low tenement house he shared with twelve other people. He explained how he bathed in fish oil and emptied his chamber pot into an alley that flowed to the Nor Loch, the body of water outside the Flodden Wall that surrounded the original city. He said that the plague of 1645 was caused by cramp and filth inside the Flodden Wall, and that the rampant disease whittled 40,000 citizens down to sixty, solving the city's problems with overcrowding.

The tour ended in a bedchamber filled with wax dummies suffering from various stages of plague. A silent figure wearing a long dark robe with a pointed hood, leather gloves, and a beak-shaped mask walked into the room. Our guide introduced him as Dr. George Ray, the famous plague doctor. As the hooded figure ministered to the wax plague victims, draining the buboes around their necks, our guide said that the doctor had filled his beak mask with broom, an herb thought to protect against the plague. The doctor didn't know the disease was carried by infected fleas; his sinister wardrobe simply guarded him against the fleas, the herbs merely masking the smell of the black ooze coming from the victims as he lanced and bled them. The guide "debunked" the popular story that the city council sealed up any plague area, sentencing its victims and their families to die inside.

"This is myth," he said, almost proudly, explaining that the victims were only quarantined in their own homes with their families. They simply had to wave a white flag outside their open window and lower a basket to someone on the street who would fill it with bread and water, sometimes a little wine. If a victim survived, she received a certificate of health and resumed a normal life.

Though mercifully short, the underground plague tour had left me feeling cold and sleepy. As we walked out into the street, I voiced a callous thought: "Well, I guess if you've seen one plague victim you've seen them all. Where to next?"

Hunter voted to go eat more haggis; Rick wanted to check out a few more whisky shops. The smell of haggis wafted from an open pub door, making my throat and stomach twitch in a bad, familiar way. I considered fleeing back to The Story Teller's Apartment, quarantining myself and waving a white flag, lowering a basket out the window, down to the street for Rick and Hunter to fill with bread and water as they passed by on their way for more haggis and whisky. But we were moving away from the Royal Mile, along a crooked street toward a crowd gathered on the sidewalk before a shop. The crowd was admiring a one hundred pound roasted pig displayed in the window, a sweet-faced shop girl who smiled and plucked side meat from the pig, mounding it on a bun, topping it all off with a slice of thick, roasted pig skin. The shop was called "Oink," and its sign boasted the house specialty, a "Delicious Crackling Hog Roast Roll." As Rick and Hunter moved through the shop door, I stepped away from the pig, assessing my limitations. I felt as if I'd been granted a certificate of health that day; it was beginning to seem possible to resume a normal life. I could not eat a crackling hog roll.

Instead, I offered to go back to the Royal Mile and book a day trip to Pitlochery, the gateway to the Highlands, a short tour that would take us through Birnam Wood, where Shakespeare set *Macbeth*. Double, double, toil and trouble, I thought. After a night of hell broth and poisoned entrails, a morning of underground filth and spectacle, I wanted only outside air, earth beneath my feet, elevation. An ancient disease requires an ancient cure--walking. After booking the tour, I walked past our apartment, beyond the World's End Close, down to the Southeast end of the Royal Mile to a park surrounding the base of a dormant volcano called Arthur's Seat. Plump, moody clouds scudded across the blue sky, and a soft breeze roused the yellow broom blazing from the volcano's lower cliffs, infusing the air with the scent of coconut. I plucked a few broom blossoms and put them in my pocket. For the rest of the trip, I carried the broom like talismans, fragrant guards against the highs and lows of Scottish cookery.

Following the Slow Black River

"Make of a nation what you will
Make of the past
What you can"

—Eavan Boland, "Anna Liffey"

THE MORNING WE ARRIVED IN DUBLIN, Rick, Hunter, and I stepped into the central atrium of the Guinness Storehouse, a room shaped like the largest pint glass in the world. We stood in the middle of a holographic stout surging down the seven-storey glass walls. The smell of hops wafted in, familiar and welcoming, like the smell of boiled peanuts sold at farmers markets back home in South Carolina. It was like standing inside a soundless, brown waterfall that churned and settled into the color of dark rubies mined from the center of the earth.

This was in late June, a week after Bloomsday, the holiday when Dubliners celebrate James Joyce by making a day-long pilgrimage along the Ulysses route through the city. Others marathon read the entire 783-page novel aloud in the pubs while drinking stout for breakfast, lunch, and dinner. On the plane over, I'd reread my favorite Joyce story, "The Dead," tracing the melancholy steps of Gabriel Conroy and his wife, Gretta, as they leave Gabriel's aunts' house on 15 Ushers Island and walk the length of the River Liffey. Having never been to Ireland, I'd planned to undertake a more modest odyssey than the Bloomsday pilgrims had taken the week before: On our first day in Ireland, my family and I would follow the slow-black tidal river, crossing the Liffey bridges, stopping for lunch in one of the historic pubs. There, Rick and I would share a pint of the "black stuff," while Hunter listened to the Irish musicians. Hunter was heading off to study music at Belmont

University in Nashville in the fall. Our first visit to Ireland would be our last trip with our son before he left for college, and began his adult life apart from us.

We'd arrived in Ireland during those rare dawn hours when the pubs close down after last call, before they reopen for breakfast. From the window of our Cork Street flat, I couldn't see the River Liffey nor could I hear any pub music. Cork Street lies silently between the Guinness Storehouse at Saint James Gate and Saint Patrick's Cathedral, in a neighborhood called "The Liberties," named so because the weavers and Huguenot refugees who first lived here were free of city taxes as well as protection from the Irish police. This was Jonathan Swift territory, where he famously threw Bibles at his impoverished parishioners who slept through his sermons and championed the rights of the most savage poor of Ireland.

The Liberties is a hardy walking distance from the historic center and the River Liffey. It was, and remains, the least elegant district of Dublin. From our flat's front window, all I could see were Neil Diamond concert posters peeling from the concrete foundations of iron-gated shops across the street from our flat. A lone Georgian building that once housed aging single women with no children to support them, the poorest of the poor, hunched on the street's only grassy lawn.

Just as my plans of following the River Liffey grew distant and unrealistic, Rick summoned me over to the back bedroom window and pointed to the view of the Guinness Storehouse. A brown brick column topped with a glass rotunda, the old factory rose above the brewers' village like a giant pint of stout with a green, glass head. The frail Irish sun rolled above the Wicklow Mountains behind the rotunda, backlighting it. I opened the window. Seagulls keened from the unseen Irish Sea. The homey opiate of hops wafted in. I imagined a newly-poured glass of this black beverage. I could almost taste its coffee and chocolate flavor hinting of iron, that creamy head on top. I felt a giddy nostalgia for Guinness stout. Though I'm not much of a drinker, especially while jet lagged at dawn, I began having a strange and urgent thirst for a morning pint. Guinness was my only craving while pregnant with Hunter. It was the first beverage I drank after I stopped nursing him. Wouldn't it be poetic justice to take him to the birthplace of Guinness before we sent him off into adulthood?

As I formed this new plan, I looked over at Hunter. He sprawled on one of the beds behind me, sinking into sleep, his calloused fingers twitching, most likely playing his beloved bass guitar in his dreams. Rick sat on the other bed, checking the bus schedule for the city center. I began campaigning to take a shorter walk over to the brewery at Saint James Gate. I grounded my claim with the fact that the Irish drink stout for breakfast, sometimes in their coffee, believing it full of iron and other nutrients. The staff members of Irish hospitals have been known to administer a pint to new mothers after they give birth in order to restore their strength.

"Guinness is like mother's milk over here," I said. "Drinking a morning pint would be like having a breakfast milkshake, chock full of local vitamins." I read aloud from the Guinness pamphlet our landlady had left for us in the flat's kitchen. I ticked off my closing arguments.

"It says here that you can spot Trinity College, Saint Patrick's Cathedral, and the Wicklow Mountains, all from the Gravity Bar at the top of the Storehouse. This will be much better than any bus tour. And you get a free pint with your ticket."

Rick looked up from his bus map. "It's kind of early," he said.

"It says that it's best to go in the morning," I said. "This way, we'll beat the crowds."

Hunter opened one eye and sat up. "Can I drink a Guinness? I researched the drinking age in Ireland on the Internet. I think it's a lot like France over here. You have to be eighteen to buy alcohol, but it's okay to drink a little if you're with your parents."

Rick and I looked at our seventeen-year-old son; neither of us had thought to research the drinking age in Ireland. Though we'd agreed to let him drink a stout while we were here with him, we hadn't planned on giving him a pint for breakfast.

I nodded carefully. "It's okay with me as long as it's okay with your father. Let's see what they say when we get there."

Standing inside the central atrium of the Guinness factory, beer surging slowly around me, I felt less urgent about making this final family trip turn out right for all of us. The Storehouse is a dark museum whose halls spiral up and around the giant pint glass at its center, its exhibits brightly lit so that you remain completely immersed in the story of Guinness, which begins with displays of its four "magic" ingredients—barley, hops, yeast, and water. We walked slowly, stopping to read every word on the narrative panels. We even sampled the barley spread over the top of a beer cask. Raked and handled by thousands of strangers before us, the slender grains tasted vaguely of roasted coffee beans.

We approached a second surge of holographic water encased in glass. Its currents emulated the "precious" water source of Guinness that trickled out of a peat bog up in the Wicklow Mountains. I began to feel lousy with mother guilt, as full of trickery as the holographic image before me. When I'd arrived at the Storehouse entrance and bought our tickets for the tour, I'd confessed to the ticket agent that my son was only seventeen, and she'd given me the family discount. Then she'd given Hunter a ticket stamped with the word "CHILD."

Hunter stood beside me, already two inches taller, dressed like the Nashville sessions man he was bent on becoming, wearing black jeans, cowboy boots, a black t-shirt with a Fender guitar on it. An overnight flight's growth of dark whiskers shadowed his pale face, his boyish features chiseled into those of a man without my noticing. His eyes followed the German and Scottish backpackers rushing by us, students just a few years older than him, who were ascending toward the Gravity Bar at the top, that green glass rotunda where they could view all of Dublin while drinking the free pint of stout that came with the cost of their ADULT tickets.

I began thinking of ways to distract my son, prolonging his inevitable disappointment. I pointed to a display called "The Art of Smelling," which read that the brewery employed coopers with good noses whose job was to sniff out foul-smelling casks unfit for reuse. If a cooper "lost his touch," he was demoted back to his regular job in the cooperage. As long as he didn't lose his sense of smell, the senior cooper could go on sniffing beer casks into his retirement until the day he died.

I nudged Hunter over to the display. "When they got really old, they would have the casks lifted to their noses by a couple of young apprentices. How would you like a job like that?"

No response. Hunter's dark eyes drifted past the modes of transportation exhibits, the trains and ships that would have enthralled him just a few years before. I followed his glance towards the Tasting Room sign. My stomach clenched, sinking as I lingered beside a German torpedo that sank one of the Guinness ships in World War I.

"Look at this," I said. "The barrels of stout on board fought their way through the hatches, keeping the ship afloat so that eight surviving members of the crew could get out. The cook said it was the barrels of beer that saved their lives."

"Of all the rooms that say stuff, this is not my favorite," Hunter said mildly.

"What is your favorite room?"

"I liked the ingredient part." He glanced toward the tasting room again.

"About that pint of Guinness—" I said.

"I'll take care of it," Rick said.

"How are you going to take care of it?" I felt my voice tighten, though I was really mad at myself, for being cheap, for breaking my promise. "I couldn't lie about his age," I whispered. "Did you want me to lie about his age? No, it's my fault. I'll take care of this."

Taking the stairs to the tasting room two at a time, I sidled up to the bar and grabbed three sample glasses shaped like miniature pints. When Rick and Hunter entered the room, I handed them each a sample. Hunter held his glass like an expert and took a long pull, as if he'd been drinking Guinness stout all his life. A slow smile blossomed across his face, and his features softened, becoming boyish again. "It is just like a morning milkshake," he said. My stomach unclenched with relief. I hadn't broken my promise, not entirely. My son had gotten a taste, if not a full pint.

The tour ended in the "pour your own perfect pint" room, where Rick and I were lined behind a bar and given a clean stout glass with the iconic minstrel harp on it. We were instructed to tip our glasses at a 45-degree angle, aiming the tap toward the harp on the glass. When the stout reached the bottom of the harp, we tilted our glasses upward.

We flipped off the tap and watched the surge, that famous mingling of air and liquid, the separation of black beer from the creamy head. As we topped off our pints, our pouring instructor cheered, "Perfect!" Holding his CHILD ticket, Hunter stood on the other side of the bar, behind the red line that separated the children from the adults. Broad shouldered and thin waisted, he looked like a fully-grown man standing among the eight, nine and ten-year-olds who also held CHILD-stamped tickets. I felt another pang of guilt as he snapped a photograph of Rick and me holding our perfect pints.

At the exit, we emerged from the museum, blinking into Dublin daylight, a foam of yellow clouds blanketing the Irish summer sun. As we walked toward the city center, I felt vaguely relieved to be out of that dark, glass-paneled building, breathing open air. I returned to my original plan of walking the length of the River Liffey, visiting the haunts of James Joyce and his characters. After that pint of morning Guinness, I didn't need to coax Rick to head toward the pub district for lunch. I suggested that we walk down to the river to eat in one of the historic taverns, listen to some traditional Irish music.

We followed a street shaped like a key that led into the city center. Passing Saint Patrick's Cathedral and Christ Church, we moved into Temple Bar, a cobbled neighborhood above the banks of the Liffey where the streets were crowded with musicians and historic pubs. We passed a tavern brimming with a victorious rugby team singing Neil Diamond's "Forever In Blue Jeans," men in gray jerseys spilling out the door to smoke and finish their pints in the streets.

We walked on. Beside the river, I discovered that we'd missed Usher's Quay and the Joyce House by several bridges. We crossed Merchant's Bridge and stood in the middle, where Joyce began Finnegans Wake in mid-sentence, "riverrun, past Eve and Adam's, from swerve of shore to bend of bay, brings us by a commodius vicus of re-circulation back to Howth Castle and environs." Disappointed in the surrounding environs, I realized that we'd started Gabriel and Gretta Conroy's famous journey in the middle rather than at the beginning. I looked down at the river. The tide was out, the black water so low I could see the bottom in places, emerald moss softening its high, dry walls. Lanky seagulls looted a three-wheeled grocery cart sinking into the muddy bottom of the once-commodious river.

The rugby team flowed towards us, a sea of gray jerseys, their voices embracing, "Love on the Rocks," as whole-heartedly as they would any Irish dirge. Before the team overtook the bridge, I snapped a quick photo of a bridge lantern, its base shaped like a mythological creature, half mermaid, half horse. It occurred to me that Joyce had left his "dear dirty Dublin" when he was only twenty-two because he found it unbearable. He had, in fact, written most of his books while in exile, recreating his hometown from memory and the letters of relatives who'd remained. This fabled city from Joyce's stories had all but disappeared. Still, I tried to rebuild it by imagining Joyce's characters, Gabriel and Gretta, walking the banks of this river at midnight during a snowfall. Gabriel brooded the loss of a different bygone era while his wife walked slightly ahead, elusive as a shadow as she mourned her childhood romance with a boy from her village who'd loved her so much he'd stood below her window in the rain the night before she moved to convent school in Dublin. Within a year, he died of consumption.

A cloud swept in from the Irish Sea, chilling the gulf-stream breeze that had warmed the air a minute before. I looked over at my son and shivered. His fair skin had turned a diaphanous white. His fatigued face looked like a death mask. Rick gave me a tired look, "Where are you going?"

I had no idea where I was going, so I tried a feeble joke. "The way to travel is to be like a meandering stream that wanders down to the ocean," I said. "This way, you don't miss anything."

Rick said he wasn't a stream when he traveled. "I don't know what kind of traveler I am, but I can tell you what I am not," he said. "I'm not the kind who thinks about the philosophy of his traveling while he's on a trip."

"I feel like I'm missing something," Hunter said.

"Me too," I said.

"No, I think we've missed it," he said. "As in, M-I-S-S, missing."

"I know," I said, understanding him perfectly.

My blood coursed with that morning pint of Guinness. I felt languid and remote, no closer to knowing Ireland than I had before my arrival that morning, and farther away from giving my son a decent send off into his adult life. Seagulls argued over dead fish lying belly up in the brackish water beneath the bridge. The rugby team crowded around us, still singing, "Love on the rocks. Ain't no surprise. Just pour me a drink. And I'll tell you some lies." So far, I'd lied to my son at the Guinness Storehouse, giving him a child's portion instead of an adult pint. I'd missed most of Joyce's famous walk along the River Liffey. But surely we hadn't missed Ireland entirely. Was my son right? Had we missed it?

We trudged against the current of rugby players, back into Temple Bar. A crowd had gathered before three musicians, and the main street was solid with listeners. The musicians were young men, barely older than Hunter, playing blues music on a mandolin and an Irish drum. The bassist played a guitar made out of an old petrol can. Hunter stopped before the band, tilting his head. I knew he was listening to the bass player as a writer reads a book, studying the language and structure of music, determining how the Irish bassist anchored the harmony, laid down the beat.

A young gypsy jumped out of the crowd. Shirtless and barefoot, he danced an unschooled jig before the musicians. The crowd cheered at first, but the boy danced for too long, without knowledge or regard for the music, until the band stopped, most likely fearing pickpockets working the street as the boy diverted the crowd's attention. Rick and I glanced at each other. I checked my purse. He checked his wallet. The crowd remained still, waiting in silence for the lovely music to begin again. But it was all over. As Rick and I pressed through the stunned crowd, Hunter dug into his pocket and fished out some change. He ran and dropped his coins into the open guitar case lying on the ground before the musicians. He returned to us, his sleepy eyes alive, excited, and I knew he'd found what he'd been missing.

In June, the sun sets in Dublin after 10 p.m. Rick and Hunter fell asleep well before sunset, and I followed them soon after. But I awoke at midnight, feeling the eerie jet-lag clarity that often comes to me in the middle of the night, in the middle of a foreign country. I'd been warned that Ireland had changed in the last two decades, that Dublin had become unrecognizably "modern," its old-world charm scarred by the Celtic Tiger, an economic boom time that clawed through the country in the mid 1990s. We'd arrived on the tail end of this movement, the week of the savage street riots in Greece, when it was rumored that the Irish economy would be the next to fall into crisis.

In theory, I understood that Ireland's prosperity had erased many aspects of its past. I also suspected that its impending economic crisis would change its present identity. At this moment, Dublin seemed in quiet flux, neither old nor young. Still, I didn't want to believe I'd missed seeing it entirely, whatever it was.

I thought it might be better to read the poetry of a living Irish writer more acquainted with this new and changing Ireland. In the morning, we'd be taking a coach tour of the Wicklow Mountains. I looked forward to seeing the source of the River Liffey, that "precious" stream that trickled out of an ancient peat bog. I'd stuffed a volume of Eavan Boland's poetry into my luggage at the last minute. I took out this book, opened it to Boland's poem about "Anna Liffey," the Celtic goddess the river is named after. Set near Boland's home at the base of the Wicklow Mountains, near the headwaters of the Liffey, the poem contemplates the flow of the river and the course of the poet's body passing into middle age. I read: "I am sure/The body of an ageing woman/Is a memory."

Outside the window, street lamps yellowed the dark leaves of trees lining Cork Street. Seagulls shrilled from the Irish Sea. Quieter and more distant in the darkness, they sounded like the memory of lost children. Beyond the light of the street lamps, the Georgian hospital that once housed aging single women sat back from the street, looking empty, outcast among the strips of characterless shops and flats. A friend once told me that the very definition of a mother is one who is left behind. Feeling a kindred void with that empty Georgian building, I filled myself with more of Boland's poetry: "Consider rivers. They are always en route to/ their own nothingness. From the first moment/ They are going home./ And so/ When language cannot do it for us,/ Cannot make us know love will not diminish us,/ There are these phrases of the ocean/ To console us."

At this raw hour, I felt reaffirmed by the poet's words. My earlier joke about traveling like a stream no longer seemed ridiculous. Here was an Irish poet saying that a woman was a stream that meandered. She was a life source on route to nothingness, her role no longer clearly defined as she discovered her children grown, naturally moving away from her at bewildering speed. Standing in Temple Bar that afternoon, listening to the street musicians, I had felt old and foolish for believing I could rebuild the historic city in my mind, as Joyce had memorialized it with words. Old Dublin was gone, and I'd felt the loss of it. But there was Hunter standing beside me, listening to the street musicians, his knowing fingers moving fluidly, plucking an invisible bass in perfect sync with the Irish bassist. Happily rapt in the musicians' blues, my son clearly understood the language of loss, but for him Ireland had been rebuilt through a single guitarist who made music out of an old petrol can. My son's ease with the foreign country he'd just entered had seemed uncanny, and comforting. After the music ended, he'd led the way out of the city center, somehow knowing the streets without knowing their names. Guided only by the spire of Saint Patrick's Cathedral, he'd led us back to our temporary home on Cork Street.

The next morning, the weather forecast predicted "warm, dry, risk of rain." This was "good" Irish weather, we were told by our guide as we stepped onto the tour coach headed for the Wicklow Mountains. A tall, ruddy Dublin native in his early sixties, our guide asked us to please call him "Young Dave." He called Hunter "Young Dog." Nobody on the bus but my family seemed to have a ticket for the tour, or to speak English, or to be on the right bus at all. Young Dave invited everyone—English and non-English speakers--to stay on board, saying, "No matter, get on the bus, we'll settle up later." I immediately liked this about him, and I anticipated more of this famous Irish hospitality.

Young Dave began the tour with an account of his day off. "Oh, mummy, it was a craicin' time at the barbecue yesterday. Me mates and I had so many pints of the black stuff that when the fire went out, all we had to do was blow on it, and it lit back up." Then, as if remembering his microphone were on, he said, "When I say craic I mean having a conversation. Speak to me. I am here for ye. Whisper in me ear, and I will tell you tings."

He drove us along the Liffey, past Trinity College and up Nassau Street, pointing out the house where James Joyce met Nora Barnacle, his wife and muse. On our way out of the city, we took a turn into District 4, the most affluent neighborhood in Dublin, where bright branches of monkey puzzle trees swooped, brushing the tops of stone walls surrounding sprawling mansions, many of them empty. Young Dave pointed out each empty mansion, asking us to guess its going price.

"Ireland is broke," he announced. "A few years ago, we were the second richest country in Europe, just beneath Amsterdam. Now we're the poorest country, just above Greece. It used to be, you couldn't get a loan. Then the banks began giving away money to anyone who walked in the doors. Now why do you suppose they did that?" he asked, looking truly puzzled. "All of me mates went out and bought cars. Now, they're all having to give them back." Then, as if to prove his point, Young Dave stopped the bus to give a ride to one of his car-less mates.

After spending an hour in the district of abandoned mansions, we drove up Brewery Road, where the government had opened a drying-out facility that was overpopulated by those driven to drink by the misfortunes of the recession.

"Imagine," Young Dave mused. "An Irishman with a drinking problem."

I was fairly certain that the abandoned mansion tour, the account of Ireland's financial collapse, and the trip up Brewery Road past the new drying-out facility were not part of the original trip. The bus stopped abruptly, and our guide interrupted his ambling conversation to curse another driver. "Bloody feckin' hell. Get out of me way or I'll skin ye alive." As we passed out of town and onto the Military Way, heading into Glencree, Young Dave stopped his talk of money and paused the bus to let a tinker wagon pass before him. His voice softened as he spoke to the tinkers, "Go on, me darlin's. Ye have the right of way."

Jolted awake by our guide's cursing and sudden mood swing, I didn't think his tour at all resembled the trip pitched at the Dublin Tourist Center, where I'd bought our tickets the day before. In fact, we'd been on the bus for at least two hours, and we hadn't yet reached the beginning of our itinerary. By now we were supposed to be winding through the mountains and glens south of Dublin, that famously green Irish countryside. I didn't mind. I was enjoying this tour guide's make-shift tour, his seeming aversion to all tourist routes and destinations, his dashing accent. Though he played up his stage Irish, his savage mood swings seemed real and unplanned. His moodiness made a dark poetic sense, his character perfectly attuned to the Irish weather and the wild countryside we were entering. Warm, dry, with a risk of rain.

Along the Military Way, the wilderness thinned. The Glencree Oaks were all destroyed by climate, or collapsed into the peat bogs. There was a strange absence of the notorious sheep that once crowded the country roads. Only white cattle grazed inside wire and neat hedges. The Great Sugar Loaf Mountain rose on our left, still beautiful, its rocky peak slop-ing into patches of bright-green pastures and belts of dark pines. Purple rhododendron blossoms flamed among the many hues of green.

We stopped beside a peat bog and unloaded in the middle of the highway to view the hand-cut turf standing on end, leaning into each other, each one a tiny brown and black monolith. Bog cotton flick-ered like stars against the gouged brown earth and green moor grasses, making it easy to imagine ancient Celtic kings appeasing their gods and other spirits by throwing human sacrifices, kegs of butter, jewels they hoped never to recover into the bogs.

When the bus sidled up beside the headwaters of the Liffey, I nearly missed them. The river's source wasn't much to look at, just an oozing tear in the brown earth stitched by chunks of gray limestone down a green slope. Young Dave didn't even stop to get off the bus at the head-waters. The source sprang from moving bogs filled with hollows, the ground around it as unstable as a sponge. He drove on to drier ground, stopping on a bridge that arched over a rocky stream spiked with yellow asphodel. We were somewhere in the Sally Gap, not at any itinerary site, but our guide thought the view beautiful, and that we should take the time to admire it while the weather was so fine. He gently commanded us to get off the bus and led us up the slope, handing us over the rocks in the stream. The heather wasn't blooming yet. All around us, it rose in brown mounds among the bright green ferns and stones.

"Imagine what this will look like in a week," Rick said. "When all this heather is blooming."

Rick and Hunter went below the bridge to search for heather blossoms while I hopped from stone to stone in the stream, settling on a long, flat one. Framed by the ancient bridge that arched between us, Hunter looked like a boy again in the distance, sitting cross-legged on a stone, calmly watching the currents shift and mingle around him. Our guide had stopped speaking, allowing us to linger inside this perfect water and soak in this quiet, poetic vista. A cloud swept over, spitting a few raindrops into my eyes. The sun continued to shine. I drug my hand in the water where it widened, becoming clear. My thoughts became spacious. Finally, I thought. This is Ireland. We didn't miss it.

After we returned from our trip, when I asked Hunter what he loved the most about Ireland, he picked up his second-hand mandolin and filled our entire house with the sound of Celtic dirges he'd overheard and memorized on the streets of Dublin, beside the River Liffey. Once, before leaving for college, he allowed me to record his playing so that I could listen to him after he was gone. Now, when the house feels unnaturally quiet without him in it, I sometimes turn on this recording. As the mandolin's voice fills the dissonant rooms of our house, I reassure myself that music, rather than words, will help him navigate his way safely into adulthood. As I sat silently inside that unnamed Wicklow stream, dragging my hand through the ancient waters, I was no longer conscious that I was beside the river's source, the beginning of the entire country. I closed my eyes, listening to the voices of my son and my husband in the distance as they rock hopped, hunting for heather just beginning to bloom. After a while, when I walked down to meet them, Rick and Hunter each placed a heather blossom into my palm. I held them like jewels recovered from the bogs.

Silent Song

In Camerota, where the locals dance salsa every night for all of summer in a club called The Cyclops, I step into the butter yellow church in the piazza and find the most sorrowful Madonna I've ever seen. She stands on the right side of the altar, her eyes red-rimmed, her young face pale, haggard, shining with sweat. Wearing a brown gown adorned with a few rustic stars, she gazes wearily toward the heavens, a hotel hand towel draped over her right arm as if she's laundered linens all day beneath Mediterranean sun. Her bare feet are bound by single black straps of leather sandals, and the sacred heart pressing down on her chest looks as heavy as the steering wheel of an ancient boat. Her crown appears as if it's been tossed to the ground beside a patch of lilies. Plucked of their white blooms, the stems rise like ditch weeds from the rocky earth around her.

There are no other visitors in San Domenico, the mother church of this town on the Cilento coast of Southern Italy. A local charwoman beats the floor with fierce, muscular strokes of a stick broom. Haloed by clipped white hair, the sweeper's face is angular and serene, barely flushed from her labor. She bears little resemblance to the woman who must have modeled for the sorrowful Madonna. The model for the statue must have been used twice, her image recycled into a second version of the Madonna placed on the left side of the altar. The second Madonna's brow has been dried of sweat, and she's adorned with lace and crown. A crowned infant Christ settles on her hip, a white ribbon tied around his wrist, a crucifix dangling from its end. This Madonna's feet are unbound from the black-strapped sandals, her toenails painted silver, but her brown eyes remain red-rimmed, weary. They look directly out, as if she knows already the weight of crown and crucifix.

The two statues of the Madonna must be effigies for all the mothers of Camerota who knew the weight of sons lost during La Miseria, a time of unimaginable poverty in early twentieth-century Italy, when seven million peasants and day laborers emigrated to North and South America, when 87% of those leaving were from Southern Italy. My own maternal grandfather, son of tenant farmers from Palermo who emigrated to the States during the depths of La Misera, when two-thirds of the island emigrated, never spoke about it directly. Whenever I asked about the country his parents left behind, he said, "C'era una volta," once upon a time. He said, "If you drop a heel of bread, you pick it up, and kiss it."

The mothers of Camerota kissed their sons before they sailed to Caracas to become thriving merchants, importing salami, olives, tinned tomatoes. Later, the mothers began fearing the bullets of political unrest in Venezuela more than famine. They feared the men would marry Venezuelan women and have children, leaving the women of Camerota to die in a paese fantasma, a ghost town filled with only the old and infirm. They called their sons home to marry Italian women. The men made several crossings in the 1940s and 50s, bringing back Spanish boats and dances, food, wives and children, South American street names and saints.

Mingled among the suffering Madonnas in the mother church are a painting of a shipwreck in a storm and statues of Saint Gerard Majella, Saint Domenico di Guzman, and Saint Louis Gonzaga. All South American men who left the safe harbors of their families to become great wandering monks in Italy, all three died of religious austerities, fatigue from excessive pilgrimages. The mother church keeps these religious figures with the collective memories of the town, its history of suffering and migrations. I've heard that this history is the reason the Italian-Venezuelans of Camerota are particularly friendly to foreigners, especially the African migrants, recent refugees from poverty and wars who've been crossing the stretch of Mediterranean between Libya and Southern Italy in what has become the world's greatest refugee crisis since the Second World War.

In April 2013, a boat carrying migrants from Eritrea, Somalia, and Ghana from Libya to Italy sank off the coast of Lampedusa, drowning over 360 people. The Italians responded by creating Mare Nostrum, which means "Our Sea," a military and humanitarian rescue operation that offered medical treatment, food, and legal aid for those seeking asylum. Though it saved an estimated 130,000 people, Mare Nostrum ended after a year, on October 31, 2014. The cash-strapped Italian government could not sustain its nine-million-euro-a-month budget. Factions of the European Union that opposed the rescue operation believed that the Italians were creating a "pull factor," encouraging more immigrants to make the dangerous sea crossing, thereby sentencing them to death at sea.

But isn't this "pull factor" only half the reason for most mass migrations? What about those who are pushed by desperate circumstances from their home countries? In November of 2014, Mare Nostrum was superseded by Operation Triton. Run by the European Border agency Frontex, Triton focuses on border patrol, and functions on a budget of three million euro a month, relying upon voluntary contributors from EU members and nonmembers, mostly smaller countries like Ireland, Portugal or Malta that feel in sympathy with the migrants and Italy.

Outside the mother church of the Italian-Venezuelan town of Camerota, June sun heats the cobblestones in the piazza. Morning swallows shriek, dodging pink bougainvillea that cloaks the arched door of a café across the piazza from the mother church. Coffee cups clank from within, and the bakery next door perfumes the air with powdered sugar. The locals dust sugar over everything they eat for breakfast: cream puffs, biscotti stuffed with almonds, hazelnuts, and citrons. They powder and slice cornetto, fill them with wildflower honey taken from bees that gather pollen from passion flowers growing on the Cape of Good Fortune, the rocky arm that embraces the marina where tipsy boats glide through swells of sapphire water into grottoes called, "Love," and, "Cathedral."

The children and grandchildren of the boatmen who crossed and re-crossed the Mediterranean have transformed themselves into merchants and artisans. On the Lungomare Trieste, the vendor's street above the marina, I step into a shop and find a case full of bracelets that look like small, silken fishing ropes. The merchant speaks in Italian peppered with Spanish, explaining how she was raised in Venezuela by a mother and grandmother who clubbed sea grasses with a baton into ropes used by sailors. Made to honor the work of the mother women in her family, the bracelets are soft, the color of dried oregano. They resemble the sea grass ropes that women in black kerchiefs stretch along cobblestones in the oil painting of old Camerota set artfully behind the bracelets.

The merchant walks me through her shop, opening each glass case filled with a lovely wonder she's fashioned with her hands. An amber necklace meant to resemble driftwood curves along a petrified piece of driftwood. Earrings the color of sapphire drape over a framed postcard of the sapphire water flowing into the opening of a local grotto. She explains how each piece of jewelry chronicles an element of her family's history, which is really the village's history of migration—the push from starvation and joblessness toward work and food in Caracas, the eventual pull back to this safe harbor in Southern Italy, where the rocky cape slopes into a good-tempered sea that endlessly cradles and carves the stone into grottoes.

Walking through her store is a little like floating through the sea grottos inside the nearby Cape of Palinuro, where sunlight siphons from chambers beneath the water, stoking it into an ethereal blue that looks like the beginning of creation. As you nudge your boat around each corner you blink and imagine wondrous shapes-- a dolphin's head or monks in prayer formed by stalagmites, a whole nativity scene sketched by water and age within walls streaked silver with sulfur. The merchant and I turn another corner in the store, and reach a case filled with necklaces strung with Chiclets. Yellow, green, orange, white, and pink stones shaped like teeth, they remind the merchant of the gum she bought from markets in Caracas when she was a child. She strings them into "treasure necklaces," hiding mother-of-pearls, polished sea glass, tiny hummingbirds and orchids carved from Italian coral between the colorful stones.

The merchant is small, sturdy. She flits to the very back of the store. There she dips head and hands into a case filled with her most treasured pieces, sleek drops of obsidian suspended within whispery thin treble clef pendants, a bracelet of lava rock moons surrounded by haloes of silver. The black jewelry blends harmoniously with the black notes on a piece of sheet music she's placed in the back of the case. The music is called "Silenzio Cantatore," Silent Song, her favorite Neapolitan barcarole, a boatman's chant whose rhythms imitate the strokes of a paddle. I read a portion of the lyrics, a sad and romantic folksong about a wounded Italian soldier on a faraway battlefield, pining for his lost love: Maria, in the silence, in the melodious silence, I don't tell you the words of love, but this sea tells you them for me!

Beside us, the window holds the mid-morning light at a distance. I realize that I'm in the presence of an artist with a talent for weaving a longing for her family's South American history with gifts from the Italian earth and sea. I realize, too, that there's no way to honor this woman's work with a significant purchase, no way to repay her for all the stories she's given me. Already, I've spent too much of her time, and I feel that I should buy something. But I've spent most of my cash at the bakery near the mother church, on a cornetto and a bag of cookies stuffed with almonds, hazelnuts, and citrons. I need to save the rest for my taxi ride back to Pisciotta, the neighboring fishing village twelve miles north where I've been living for the last week.

I have enough change for a postcard. I select one that looks like an oil painting of a scene from old Camerota called "Lavorazione dell' erba," herb work. In it, a woman sits on a wooden bench beside the old taverna, holding a baton over a bundle of grasses. Surely this muscle work was heavy and unending. Signs of La Miseria surround her, yet she's much more beautiful than the haunted Madonnas inside the mother church. Her body softened and aged by motherhood, her abundant breasts hang loose inside her rustic blouse, and her legs are swathed in a pale blue skirt that's ripped down one side. The harsh sun has darkened her neck and arms into the deep brown of her baton. Her bare toes curl comfortably in the dirt beside the stone as she gazes at the grasses she's about to pound. Her face is burnished, as if lit from within by the belief in the usefulness of her work.

I buy the postcard. The merchant smiles, begins rooting around in a basket on the floor beside the cash register. She studies me, then sifts through the shells, picking up one after another, discarding several more before she pulls out an alphabet cone shell, mottled brown and white, the slender opening along its side a deep coral pink.

"I want you to have something from here," she says. "For listening."

On the way back to Pisciotta, I talk to the taxi driver, Mimmo, a native of Camerota. Tall and barrel-chested, his face looks as if it were chiseled from one of the local cliffs. He's transformed his own car into a taxi, and hung a tiny green gym shoe from his rearview mirror along with his cab license. For the price of a two-way cab fare, he's tossed in a personal tour of his hometown. The green shoe swings wildly as he drives the winding road between sea and cliffs, one hand on the steering wheel, the other pointing out all the beaches, bays and natural arches we speed past. "Guarda!" he says. Behold! As he relates, the beaches of Camerota are the cleanest in the region. The bays are the deepest. The natural arches are the highest. Above all, I must return that evening to dance the salsa all night long at the Cyclops Club because it will be the most fun I'll have my entire time in Italy.

I explain that I won't be returning to dance the salsa that night. This disappointing news silences him for a moment, so I show him the postcard of the herb worker with hopes of reviving the conversation. "My Babo did this." He explains that his mother was from Venezuela, that she clubbed grasses into fishing ropes in the harbor like the woman in the postcard.

Just outside Camerota, Mimmo halts the cab, and picks up a young woman walking along the road. She's African, a recent migrant. She's walking away from Camerota, wearing the uniform of a domestic, heading toward a few holiday villas in the neighboring hills above and below Pisciotta. A guest worker, the girl lives safely away from the barely habitable reception centers farther south in Italy and Sicily. Still, she has at least ten more miles to walk before she reaches Pisciotta, and it's the Mezzogiorno, the hottest part of mid-day, when the locals lock up shops and cafès in order to drowse through the heat.

Mimmo offers robustly, but the girl argues gently with him in fluent Italian accented with French. He wants to give her a free ride all the way into Pisciotta. She refuses with a laugh and a firm, "No, I can walk the rest of the way." As the Italian cab driver and the African girl argue amiably for another mile, I sense that Mimmo feels bound by the same history of migration. I sense that the girl feels less of this affinity with

Mimmo, much less at home here. When we reach a fork in the road, the girl wins the argument, and Mimmo releases her from the cab.

The road to the left is an easy coastline road that leads down to the Marina of Pisciotta; the road to the right climbs an incline toward the town's historic center that lies near the summit 650 feet above. The girl closes the taxi door, heading right, climbing the road up the cliff. I suspect that she'll clean houses all afternoon and evening, and maybe walk the road back to Camerota after dark.

We continue driving. Mimmo casts fatherly glances through the rearview mirror until he no longer can see the girl. When she disappears entirely, Mimmo shakes his head, his broad shoulders hunched in defeat and bewilderment.

"That was very kind," I say.

"Kindness is not expensive," he says. "What does it ever cost to be kind?"

According to the International Organization for Migration, in the year after Mare Nostrum was replaced by the less-generously funded Triton Operation, deaths at sea between Africa and Southern Italy rose nine times. In April 2015, an Italian naval ship attempted to rescue a boat packed with 800 migrants. Those on the upper deck leaned toward the Italian ship, and capsized their own boat. Twenty-eight survivors were pulled from a sea of bodies. The dead not found in the water were discovered locked in the boat's lower hold.

Thousands of migrants continue to arrive daily from such places as Algeria, Egypt, Somalia, Niger, Senegal, Mali, Zambia, and Ghana. Many have been forced onto death trap boats at gunpoint by smugglers working the ports of Libya. The concrete reception centers on Lampedusa and in Calabria bulge with migrants who await papers, jobs and housing in more affluent cities in Northern Europe. The harbors of Sicily and some towns on the Southern-most coast of Italy have become graveyards of splintered, unseaworthy boats.

Now that I've spent a day among the lively migrants of Camerota, the medieval village of Pisciotta looks as still and ethereal as a ghost town tucked into a swath of olive groves near the cliff's summit. Mimmo and I drive the rest of the way in silence, and he drops me off in the empty piazza. In my room, I sit near its only window overlooking the terracotta rooftops of villas sleeping within the silvery-green olive trees lacing the cliff that slopes to the sea. I pull out the shell given to me by the merchant of Camerota. I've since read that the snails that live within this sort of shell use a venomous tooth to harpoon and paralyze their prey. It's best to handle the live ones with care. Now emptied and removed from the sea, it's a perfect cone, its slender opening the color of a healthy ear. I run my finger through it, wondering if the unspeakable dangers from the African girl's past have left her unable to accept the present kindness from the Italian taxi driver. Was it the "push" from her home country or the "pull" of Italy that brought her here? Wouldn't it be better to think of the Mediterranean again as "our sea," rather than a plank of lethal water between Libya and Italy that must be policed? How much would it cost if more, and more affluent, countries from around the world reached out a kind hand to assist this historically cash-poor region of a single, small country in the European Union?

I watch the lapis blue swells from the deep push toward the pale green shallows near the harbor, mingling, pulling the weaker water back into the sea. If the sea is telling me the answers to any of my questions, I'm too far above the shore to hear it. Instead I hear the Breath of Africa, a wind that blows through the villages of Southern Italy in summer, casting a spell of melodious silence once believed by ancient mariners to be the song of sirens.

Winter's Work

MY FATHER SENDS ME A PHOTO of two deer tunneling through four feet of
Ohio snow. Their faces float as if they tread a lake of milk spilled across
his backyard. All winter my father has photographed snow through ice-
slicked pines barring the window of the bedroom where he ministers to
my mother as she drifts into dementia, her mind dropping street names,
how to use a fork, her left foot, and right. Before she forgot walking, she
ran away, down the switchback road beside their house. My father found
her barefoot, dressed only in a nightgown, face down in a snowdrift
searching for her toothbrush. He will not leave her for an instant. He
brings her toothbrushes bundled into bouquets, romance novels poured
into a Hefty bag by his oldest sister, the maiden aunt who toiled beside
my grandmother in a garden gated by wild muscadine, an unromantic
life my mother always hated.

One Easter, during a late snow, my father and I escaped the dishwa-
ter steam of my grandmother's kitchen, my aunt and mother working,
plucking ham bones beneath palm fronds lashed behind Christ's cruci-
fixion. We walked to the Catholic church that ended the road. A ringing
bell knocked an ice boulder from the steeple. Loose shards splintered
my face. To distract me from the sting, my father took my hand, led me
back through woods behind the houses, pointing to a doe's footprints
marching a single row through light powder.

Forty springs later, he tells me over the phone, "You can shovel it
out of one place, but it's got to settle somewhere else." He's speaking
of the snow piling in their driveway, but I'm reminded of plaque settling
over the briar of dying blood vessels in my mother's mind, osteoporo-
sis powdering her pelvis, splintering her arm bone from shoulder ball,
splitting her wrist down to ring finger, her nerve endings so deadened
by disease that the doctors pull her abscessed teeth without anesthesia.

My father confides that it doesn't hurt when she hits him, that she
no longer knows him in the bedroom's darkness as he kisses her good
night. He says the doctor wants to drug what's left of her, a last-resort
term called "snowing under." I think of avalanches tumbling across the

slick road to my parent's house. My turn to distract my father, I search for back routes, knowing there's no bypassing the going of my mother's mind, or her body's flinty skid into stillness. I drive through Carolina mountains whose spines bristle with black pitch pine. The winter sky is a starched sheet chafing all that lies naked and devoted beneath it.

About the Author

Susan Tekulve is the author of *In the Garden of Stone*, winner of the 2012 South Carolina First Novel Prize and a 2014 Gold IPPY Award. She's also published two short story collections: *Savage Pilgrims* and *My Mother's War Stories*. Her stories and essays have appeared in *Shenandoah, The Georgia Review, New Letters, Best New Writing 2007, The Indiana Review, Denver Quarterly, Puerto del Sol, Prairie Schooner, North Dakota Quarterly, Connecticut Review, Beloit Fiction Journal, Crab Orchard Review, The Literary Review, Web Del Sol, Black Warrior Review,* and *The Kansas City Star.* She has been awarded a Sewanee Writers' Conference Scholarship and a Bread Loaf Writers' Conference Scholarship. An Associate Professor of English, she teaches in the BFA and MFA in creative writing programs at Converse College.

www.ingramcontent.com/pod-product-compliance
Lightning Source LLC
Chambersburg PA
CBHW020916180626
46816CB00007BA/2426